THE DIGITAL REVOLUTION

ARVIND UPADHYAY

This book is about the failure of companies to stay atop their industries when they confront certain types of market and technological change. It's not about the failure of simply any company, but of good companies—the kinds that many managers have admired and tried to emulate, the companies known for their abilities to innovate and execute. Companies stumble for many reasons, of course, among them bureaucracy, arrogance, tired executive blood, poor planning, short-term investment horizons, inadequate skills and resources, and just plain bad luck. But this book is not about companies with such weaknesses: It is about well-managed companies that have their competitive antennae up, listen astutely to their customers, invest aggressively in new technologies, and yet still lose market dominance. Such seemingly unaccountable failures happen in industries that move fast and in those that move slow; in those built on electronics technology and those built on chemical and mechanical technology; in manufacturing and in service industries. Sears Roebuck, for example, was regarded for decades as one of the most astutely managed retailers in the world. At its zenith Sears accounted for more than 2 percent of all retail sales in the United States. It pioneered several innovations critical to the success of today's most admired retailers: for example, supply chain management, store brands, catalogue retailing, and credit card sales. The esteem in which Sears' management was held shows in this 1964 excerpt from Fortune: "How did Sears do it? In a way, the most arresting aspect of its story is that there was no gimmick. Sears opened no big bag of tricks, shot off no skyrockets. Instead, it looked as though everybody in its organization simply did the right thing, easily and naturally. And their cumulative effect was to create an extraordinary powerhouse of a company."[1] Yet no one speaks about Sears that way today. Somehow, it completely missed the advent of discount retailing and home centers. In the midst of today's catalogue retailing boom, Sears has been driven from that business. Indeed, the very viability of its retailing operations has been questioned. One commentator has noted that "Sears' Merchandise Group lost $1.3 billion (in 1992) even before a $1.7 billion restructuring charge. Sears let arrogance blind it to basic changes taking place in the American marketplace."[2] Another writer has complained, Sears has been a disappointment for investors who have watched its stock sink dismally in the face of unkept promises of a turnaround. Sears' old merchandising approach—a vast, middle-of-the-road array of mid-priced goods and services—is no longer competitive. No question, the constant disappointments, the repeated predictions of a turnaround that never seems to come, have reduced the credibility of Sears' management in both the financial and merchandising communities. 3 It is striking to note that Sears received its accolades at exactly the time—in the mid-1960s—when it was ignoring the rise of discount retailing and home centers, the lower-cost formats for marketing name-brand hard goods that ultimately stripped Sears of its core franchise. Sears was praised as one of the best-managed companies in the world at the very time it let Visa and MasterCard usurp the enormous lead it had established in the use of credit cards in retailing. In some industries this pattern of leadership failure has been repeated more than once. Consider the computer industry. IBM dominated the mainframe market but missed by years the emergence of minicomputers, which were technologically much simpler than mainframes. In fact, no other major manufacturer of mainframe computers became a significant player in the minicomputer business.

Digital Equipment Corporation created the minicomputer market and was joined by a set of other aggressively managed companies: Data General, Prime, Wang, Hewlett-Packard, and Nixdorf. But each of these companies in turn missed the desktop personal computer market. It was left to Apple Computer, together with Commodore, Tandy, and IBM's stand-alone PC division, to create the personal-computing market. Apple, in particular, was uniquely innovative in establishing the standard for user-friendly computing. But Apple and IBM lagged five years behind the leaders in bringing portable computers to market. Similarly, the firms that built the engineering workstation market— Apollo, Sun, and Silicon Graphics—were all newcomers to the industry. As in retailing, many of these leading computer manufacturers were at one time regarded as among the best-managed companies in the world and were held up by journalists and scholars of management as examples for all to follow. Consider this assessment of Digital Equipment, made in 1986: "Taking on Digital Equipment Corp. these days is like standing in front of a moving train. The $7.6 billion computer maker has been gathering speed while most rivals are stalled in a slump in the computer industry."4 The author proceeded to warn IBM to watch out, because it was standing on the tracks. Indeed, Digital was one of the most prominently featured companies in the McKinsey study that led to the book In Search of Excellence. 5 Yet a few years later, writers characterized DEC quite differently: Digital Equipment Corporation is a company in need of triage. Sales are drying up in its key minicomputer line. A two-year-old restructuring plan has failed miserably. Forecasting and production planning systems have failed miserably. Cost-cutting hasn't come close to restoring profitability. . . . But the real misfortune may be DEC's lost opportunities. It has squandered two years trying halfway measures to respond to the low-margin personal computers and workstations that have transformed the computer industry.6 In Digital's case, as in Sears, the very decisions that led to its decline were made at the time it was so widely regarded as being an astutely managed firm. It was praised as a paragon of managerial excellence at the very time it was ignoring the arrival of the desktop computers that besieged it a few years later. Sears and Digital are in noteworthy company. Xerox long dominated the market for plain paper photocopiers used in large, high-volume copying centers. Yet it missed huge growth and profit opportunities in the market for small tabletop photocopiers, where it became only a minor player. Although steel minimills have now captured 40 percent of the North American steel market, including nearly all of the region's markets for bars, rods, and structural steel, not a single integrated steel company—American, Asian, or European—had by 1995 built a plant using minimill technology. Of the thirty manufacturers of cable-actuated power shovels, only four survived the industry's twenty-fiveyear transition to hydraulic excavation technology. As we shall see, the list of leading companies that failed when confronted with disruptive changes in technology and market structure is a long one. At first glance, there seems to be no pattern in the changes that overtook them. In some cases the new technologies swept through quickly; in others, the transition took decades. In some, the new technologies were complex and expensive to develop. In others, the deadly technologies were simple extensions of what the leading companies already did better than anyone else. One theme common to all of these failures, however, is that the decisions that led to failure were made when the leaders in question were widely regarded as among the best companies in the world. 9 There are two ways to resolve this paradox. One might be to conclude that firms such as Digital, IBM, Apple, Sears, Xerox, and Bucyrus Erie must never have been well managed. Maybe they were successful because of good luck and fortuitous timing, rather than good management. Maybe they finally fell on hard times because their good fortune ran out. Maybe. An alternative explanation, however, is that these failed firms were as well-run as one could expect a firm managed by mortals to be—but that there is something about the way decisions get made in successful organizations that sows the seeds of eventual failure. The research reported in this book supports this latter view: It shows that in the cases of well-managed firms such as those cited above, good management was the most powerful reason they failed to stay atop their industries. Precisely because these firms listened to their customers, invested aggressively in new technologies that would provide their customers more and better products of the sort they wanted, and because they carefully studied market trends and systematically allocated investment capital to innovations that promised the best returns, they lost their positions of leadership. What this implies at a deeper level is that many of what are now widely accepted principles of good management are, in fact, only situationally appropriate. There are times at which it is right not to listen to customers, right to invest in developing lower-performance products that promise lower margins, and right to aggressively pursue small, rather than substantial, markets. This book derives a set of rules, from carefully designed research and analysis of innovative successes and failures in the disk drive and other industries, that managers can use to judge when the widely accepted principles of good management should be followed and when alternative principles are appropriate. These rules, which I call principles of disruptive innovation, show that when good companies fail, it often has been because their managers either ignored these principles or chose to fight them. Managers can be extraordinarily effective in managing even the most difficult innovations if they work to understand and harness the principles of disruptive innovation. As in many of life's most challenging endeavors, there is great value in coming to grips with "the way the world works," and in managing innovative efforts in ways that accommodate such forces. The Innovator's Dilemma is intended to help a wide range of managers, consultants, and academics in manufacturing and service businesses—high tech or low—in slowly evolving or rapidly changing environments. Given that aim, technology, as used in this book, means the processes by which an organization transforms labor, capital, materials, and information into products and services of greater value. All firms have technologies. A retailer like Sears employs a particular technology to procure, present, sell, and deliver products to its customers, while a discount warehouse retailer like PriceCostco employs a different technology. This concept of technology therefore extends beyond engineering and manufacturing to encompass a range of marketing, investment, and managerial processes. Innovation refers to a change in one of these technologies.

To establish the theoretical depth of the ideas in this book, the breadth of their usefulness, and their applicability to the future as well as the past, I have divided this book into two parts. Part One, chapters 1 through 4, builds a framework that explains why sound decisions by great managers can lead firms to failure. The picture these chapters paint is truly that of an innovator's dilemma: the logical, competent decisions of management that are critical to the success of their companies are also the reasons why they lose their positions of leadership. Part Two, chapters 5 through 10, works to resolve the dilemma. Building on our understanding of why and under what circumstances new technologies have caused great firms to fail, it prescribes managerial solutions to the dilemma—how executives can simultaneously do what is right for the near-term health of their established businesses, while focusing adequate resources on the disruptive technologies that ultimately could lead to their downfall.

WHY GOOD MANAGEMENT CAN LEAD TO FAILURE The failure framework is built upon three findings from this study. The first is that there is a strategically important distinction between what I call sustaining technologies and those that are disruptive. These concepts are very different from the incremental-versus-radical distinction that has characterized many studies of this problem. Second, the pace of technological progress can, and often does, outstrip what markets need. This means that the relevance and competitiveness of different technological approaches can change with respect to different markets over time. And third, customers and financial structures of successful companies color heavily the sorts of investments that appear to be attractive to them, relative to certain types of entering firms. Sustaining versus Disruptive Technologies.

Most new technologies foster improved product performance. I call these sustaining technologies. Some sustaining technologies can be discontinuous or radical in character, while others are of an incremental nature. What all sustaining technologies have in common is that they improve the performance of established products, along the dimensions of performance that mainstream customers in major markets have historically valued. Most technological advances in a given industry are sustaining in character. An important finding revealed in this book is that rarely have even the most radically difficult sustaining technologies precipitated the failure of leading firms. Occasionally, however, disruptive technologies emerge: innovations that result in worse product performance, at least in the near-term. Ironically, in each of the instances studied in this book, it was disruptive technology that precipitated the leading firms' failure. Disruptive technologies bring to a market a very different value proposition than had been available previously. Generally, disruptive technologies underperform established products in mainstream markets. But they have other features that a few fringe (and generally new) customers value. Products based on disruptive technologies are typically cheaper, simpler, smaller, and, frequently, more convenient to use. There are many examples in addition to the personal desktop computer and discount retailing examples cited above. Small off-road motorcycles introduced in North America and Europe by Honda, Kawasaki, and Yamaha were disruptive technologies relative to the powerful, over-the-road cycles made by Harley-Davidson and BMW. Transistors were disruptive technologies relative to vacuum tubes. Health maintenance organizations were disruptive technologies to conventional health insurers. In the near future, "internet appliances" may become disruptive technologies to suppliers of personal computer hardware and software. Trajectories of Market Need versus Technology Improvement The second element of the failure framework, the observation that technologies can progress faster than market demand, illustrated in Figure I.1, means that in their efforts to provide better products than their competitors and earn higher prices and margins, suppliers often "overshoot" their market: They give customers more than they need or ultimately are willing to pay for. And more importantly, it means that disruptive technologies that may underperform today, relative to what users in the market demand, may be fully performance-competitive in that same market tomorrow. Many who once needed mainframe computers for their data processing requirements, for example, no longer need or buy mainframes. Mainframe performance has surpassed the requirements of many original customers, who today find that much of what they need to do can be done on desktop machines linked to file servers. In other words, the needs of many computer users have increased more slowly than the rate of improvement provided by computer designers. Similarly, many shoppers who in 1965 felt they had to shop at department stores to be assured of quality and selection now satisfy those needs quite well at Target and Wal-Mart.

Disruptive Technologies versus Rational Investments The last element of the failure framework, the conclusion by established companies that investing aggressively in disruptive technologies is not a rational financial decision for them to make, has three bases. First, disruptive products are simpler and cheaper; they generally promise lower margins, not greater profits. Second, disruptive technologies typically are first commercialized in emerging or insignificant markets. And third, leading firms' most profitable customers generally don't want, and indeed initially can't use, products based on disruptive technologies. By and large, a disruptive technology is initially embraced by the least profitable customers in a market. Hence, most companies with a practiced discipline of listening to their best customers and identifying new products that promise greater profitability and growth are rarely able to build a case for investing in disruptive technologies until it is too late. TESTING THE FAILURE FRAMEWORK This book defines the problem of disruptive technologies and describes how they can be managed, taking care to establish what researchers call the internal and external validity of its propositions. Chapters 1 and 2 develop the failure framework in the context of the disk drive industry, and the initial pages of chapters 4 through 8 return to that industry to build a progressively deeper understanding of why disruptive technologies are such vexatious phenomena for good managers to confront successfully. The reason for painting such a complete picture of a single industry is to establish the internal validity of the failure framework. If a framework or model cannot reliably explain what happened within a single industry, it cannot be applied to other situations with confidence. Chapter 3 and the latter sections of chapters 4 through 9 are structured to explore the external validity of the failure framework—the conditions in which we might expect the framework to yield useful insights. Chapter 3 uses the framework to examine why the leading makers of cable excavators were driven from the earthmoving market by makers of hydraulic machines, and chapter 4 discusses why the world's integrated steel makers have floundered in the face of minimill technology. Chapter 5 uses the model to examine the success of discount retailers, relative to conventional chain and department stores, and to probe the impact of disruptive technologies in the motor control and printer industries. 13 Chapter 6 examines the emerging personal digital assistant industry and reviews how the electric motor control industry was upended by disruptive technology. Chapter 7 recounts how entrants using disruptive technologies in motorcycles and logic circuitry dethroned industry leaders; chapter 8 shows how and why computer makers fell victim to disruption; and chapter 9 spotlights the same phenomena in the accounting software and insulin businesses. Chapter 10 applies the framework to a case study of the electric vehicle, summarizing the lessons learned from the other industry studies, showing how they can be used to assess the opportunity and threat of electric vehicles, and describing how they might be applied to make an electric vehicle commercially successful. Chapter 11 summarizes the book's findings. Taken in sum, these chapters present a theoretically strong, broadly valid, and managerially practical framework for understanding disruptive technologies and how they have precipitated the fall from industry leadership of some of history's best-managed companies. HARNESSING THE PRINCIPLES OF DISRUPTIVE INNOVATION Colleagues who have read my academic papers reporting the findings recounted in chapters 1 through 4 were struck by their near-fatalism. If good management practice drives the failure of successful firms faced with disruptive technological change, then the usual answers to companies' problems—planning better, working harder, becoming more customer-driven, and taking a longer-term perspective—all exacerbate the problem. Sound execution, speed-to-market, total quality management, and process reengineering are similarly ineffective. Needless to say, this is disquieting news to people who teach future managers! Chapters 5 through 10, however, suggest that although the solution to disruptive technologies cannot be found in the standard tool kit of good management, there are, in fact, sensible ways to deal effectively with this challenge. Every company in every industry works under certain forces—laws of organizational nature—that act powerfully to define what that company can and cannot do. Managers faced with disruptive technologies fail their companies when these forces overpower them. By analogy, the ancients who attempted to fly by strapping feathered wings to their arms and flapping with all their might as they leapt from high places invariably failed. Despite their dreams and hard work, they were fighting against some very powerful forces of nature. No one could be strong enough to win this fight. Flight became possible only after people came to understand the relevant natural laws and principles that defined how the world worked: the law of gravity, Bernoulli's principle, and the concepts of lift, drag, and resistance. When people then designed flying systems that recognized or harnessed the power of these laws and principles, rather than fighting them, they were finally able to fly to heights and distances that were previously unimaginable. The objective of chapters 5 through 10 is to propose the existence of five laws or principles of disruptive technology. As in the analogy with manned flight, these laws are so strong that managers who ignore or fight them are nearly powerless to pilot their companies through a disruptive technology storm. These chapters show, however, that if managers can understand and harness these forces, rather than fight them, they can in fact succeed spectacularly when confronted with disruptive technological change. I am particularly anxious that managers read these chapters for understanding, rather than for simple answers. I am very confident that the great managers about whom this book is written will be very capable on their own of finding the answers that best fit their circumstances. But they must first 14 understand what has caused those circumstances and what forces will affect the feasibility of their solutions. The following paragraphs summarize these principles and what managers can do to harness or accommodate them. Principle #1:

Companies Depend on Customers and Investors for Resources The history of the disk drive industry shows that the established firms stayed atop wave after wave of sustaining technologies (technologies that their customers needed), while consistently stumbling over simpler disruptive ones. This evidence supports the theory of resource dependence. 7 Chapter 5 summarizes this theory, which states that while managers may think they control the flow of resources in their firms, in the end it is really customers and investors who dictate how money will be spent because companies with investment patterns that don't satisfy their customers and investors don't survive. The highest-performing companies, in fact, are those that are the best at this, that is, they have well-developed systems for killing ideas that their customers don't want. As a result, these companies find it very difficult to invest adequate resources in disruptive technologies—lower-margin opportunities that their customers don't want—until their customers want them. And by then it is too late. Chapter 5 suggests a way for managers to align or harness this law with their efforts to confront disruptive technology. With few exceptions, the only instances in which mainstream firms have successfully established a timely position in a disruptive technology were those in which the firms' managers set up an autonomous organization charged with building a new and independent business around the disruptive technology. Such organizations, free of the power of the customers of the mainstream company, ensconce themselves among a different set of customers—those who want the products of the disruptive technology. In other words, companies can succeed in disruptive technologies when their managers align their organizations with the forces of resource dependence, rather than ignoring or fighting them. The implication of this principle for managers is that, when faced with a threatening disruptive technology, people and processes in a mainstream organization cannot be expected to allocate freely the critical financial and human resources needed to carve out a strong position in the small, emerging market. It is very difficult for a company whose cost structure is tailored to compete in high-end markets to be profitable in low-end markets as well. Creating an independent organization, with a cost structure honed to achieve profitability at the low margins characteristic of most disruptive technologies, is the only viable way for established firms to harness this principle. Principle #2: Small

Markets Don't Solve the Growth Needs of Large Companies Disruptive technologies typically enable new markets to emerge. There is strong evidence showing that companies entering these emerging markets early have significant first-mover advantages over later entrants. And yet, as these companies succeed and grow larger, it becomes progressively more difficult for them to enter the even newer small markets destined to become the large ones of the future. 15 To maintain their share prices and create internal opportunities for employees to extend the scope of their responsibilities, successful companies need to continue to grow. But while a $40 million company needs to find just $8 million in revenues to grow at 20 percent in the subsequent year, a $4 billion company needs to find $800 million in new sales. No new markets are that large. As a consequence, the larger and more successful an organization becomes, the weaker the argument that emerging markets can remain useful engines for growth. Many large companies adopt a strategy of waiting until new markets are "large enough to be interesting." But the evidence presented in chapter 6 shows why this is not often a successful strategy. Those large established firms that have successfully seized strong positions in the new markets enabled by disruptive technologies have done so by giving responsibility to commercialize the disruptive technology to an organization whose size matched the size of the targeted market. Small organizations can most easily respond to the opportunities for growth in a small market. The evidence is strong that formal and informal resource allocation processes make it very difficult for large organizations to focus adequate energy and talent on small markets, even when logic says they might be big someday. Principle #3: Markets that Don't Exist Can't Be Analyzed Sound market research and good planning followed by execution according to plan are hallmarks of good management. When applied to sustaining technological innovation, these practices are invaluable; they are the primary reason, in fact, why established firms led in every single instance of sustaining innovation in the history of the disk drive industry. Such reasoned approaches are feasible in dealing with sustaining technology because the size and growth rates of the markets are generally known, trajectories of technological progress have been established, and the needs of leading customers have usually been well articulated. Because the vast majority of innovations are sustaining in character, most executives have learned to manage innovation in a sustaining context, where analysis and planning were feasible. In dealing with disruptive technologies leading to new markets, however, market researchers and business planners have consistently dismal records. In fact, based upon the evidence from the disk drive, motorcycle, and microprocessor industries, reviewed in chapter 7, the only thing we may know for sure when we read experts' forecasts about how large emerging markets will become is that they are wrong. In many instances, leadership in sustaining innovations—about which information is known and for which plans can be made—is not competitively important. In such cases, technology followers do about as well as technology leaders. It is in disruptive innovations, where we know least about the market, that there are such strong first-mover advantages. This is the innovator's dilemma. Companies whose investment processes demand quantification of market sizes and financial returns before they can enter a market get paralyzed or make serious mistakes when faced with disruptive technologies. They demand market data when none exists and make judgments based upon financial projections when neither revenues or costs can, in fact, be known. Using planning and marketing techniques that were developed to manage sustaining technologies in the very different context of disruptive ones is an exercise in flapping wings. 16 Chapter 7 discusses a different approach to strategy and planning that recognizes the law that the right markets, and the right strategy for exploiting them, cannot be known in advance. Called discoverybased planning, it suggests that managers assume that forecasts are wrong, rather than right, and that the strategy they have chosen to pursue may likewise be wrong. Investing and managing under such assumptions drives managers to develop plans for learning what needs to be known, a much more effective way to confront disruptive technologies successfully. Principle #4: An Organization's Capabilities Define Its Disabilities When managers tackle an innovation problem, they instinctively work to assign capable people to the job. But once they've found the right people, too many managers then assume that the organization in which they'll work will also be capable of succeeding at the task. And that is dangerous—because organizations have capabilities that exist independently of the people who work within them. An organization's capabilities reside in two places. The first is in its processes—the methods by which people have learned to transform inputs of labor, energy, materials, information, cash, and technology into outputs of higher value. The second is in the organization's values, which are the criteria that managers and employees in the organization use when making prioritization decisions. People are quite flexible, in that they can be trained to succeed at quite different things. An employee of IBM, for example, can quite readily change the way he or she works, in order to work successfully in a small start-up company. But processes and values are not flexible. A process that is effective at managing the design of a minicomputer, for example, would be ineffective at managing the design of a desktop personal computer. Similarly, values that cause employees to prioritize projects to develop high-margin products, cannot simultaneously accord priority to low-margin products. The very processes and values that constitute an organization's capabilities in one context, define its disabilities in another context. Chapter 8 will present a framework that can help a manager understand precisely where in his or her organization its capabilities and disabilities reside. Drawing on studies in the disk drive and computer industries, it offers tools that managers can use to create new capabilities, when the processes and values of the present organization would render it incapable of successfully addressing a new problem. Principle #5: Technology Supply May Not Equal Market Demand Disruptive technologies, though they initially can only be used in small markets remote from the mainstream, are disruptive because they subsequently can become fully performance-competitive within the mainstream market against established products. As depicted in Figure I.1, this happens because the pace of technological progress in products frequently exceeds the rate of performance improvement that mainstream customers demand or can absorb. As a consequence, products whose features and functionality closely match market needs today often follow a trajectory of improvement by which they overshoot mainstream market needs tomorrow. And products that seriously underperform today, relative to customer expectations in mainstream markets, may become directly performance-competitive tomorrow. Chapter 9 shows that when this happens, in markets as diverse as disk drives, accounting software, and diabetes care, the basis of competition—the criteria by which customers choose one product over 17 another—changes. When the performance of two or more competing products has improved beyond what the market demands, customers can no longer base their choice upon which is the higher performing product. The basis of product choice often evolves from functionality to reliability, then to convenience, and, ultimately, to price. Many students of business have described phases of the product life cycle in various ways. But chapter 9 proposes that the phenomenon in which product performance overshoots market demands is the primary mechanism driving shifts in the phases of the product life cycle. In their efforts to stay ahead by developing competitively superior products, many companies don't realize the speed at which they are moving up-market, over-satisfying the needs of their original customers as they race the competition toward higher-performance, higher-margin markets. In doing so, they create a vacuum at lower price points into which competitors employing disruptive technologies can enter. Only those companies that carefully measure trends in how their mainstream customers use their products can catch the points at which the basis of competition will change in the markets they serve. LESSONS FOR SPOTTING DISRUPTIVE THREATS AND OPPORTUNITIES Some managers and researchers familiar with these ideas have arrived at this point in the story in an anxious state because the evidence is very strong that even the best managers have stumbled badly when their markets were invaded by disruptive technologies. Most urgently, they want to know whether their own businesses are targets for an attacking disruptive technologist and how they can defend their business against such an attack before it is too late. Others, interested in finding entrepreneurial opportunities, wonder how they can identify potentially disruptive technologies around which new companies and markets can be built. Chapter 10 addresses these questions in a rather unconventional way. Rather than offering a checklist of questions to ask or analyses to perform, it creates a case study of a particularly vexing but wellknown problem in technological innovation: the electric vehicle. Positioning myself in the role of protagonist—as the program manager responsible for electric vehicle development in a major automobile manufacturing company wrestling with the mandate of the California Air Resources Board to begin selling electric vehicles in that state—I explore the question of whether electric vehicles are in fact a disruptive technology and then suggest ways to organize this program, set its strategy, and manage it to succeed. In the spirit of all case studies, the purpose of this chapter is not to advance what I believe to be the correct answer to this innovator's challenge. Rather, it suggests a methodology and a way of thinking about the problem of managing disruptive technological change that should prove useful in many other contexts. Chapter 10 thus takes us deeply into the innovator's dilemma that "good" companies often begin their descent into failure by aggressively investing in the products and services that their most profitable customers want. No automotive company is currently threatened by electric cars, and none contemplates a wholesale leap into that arena. The automobile industry is healthy. Gasoline engines have never been more reliable. Never before has such high performance and quality been available at such low prices. Indeed, aside from governmental mandates, there is no reason why we should expect the established car makers to pursue electric vehicles.

But the electric car is a disruptive technology and potential future threat. The innovator's task is to ensure that this innovation—the disruptive technology that doesn't make sense—is taken seriously within the company without putting at risk the needs of present customers who provide profit and growth. As chapter 10 concretely lays out, the problem can be resolved only when new markets are considered and carefully developed around new definitions of value—and when responsibility for building the business is placed within a focused organization whose size and interest are carefully aligned with the unique needs of the market's customers.

Contents

1

Insights from the Hard Disk Drive Industry

When I began my search for an answer to the puzzle of why the best firms can fail, a friend offered some sage advice. "Those who study genetics avoid studying humans," he noted. "Because new generations come along only every thirty years or so, it takes a long time to understand the cause and effect of any changes. Instead, they study fruit flies, because they are conceived, born, mature, and die all within a single day. If you want to understand why something happens in business, study the disk drive industry. Those companies are the closest things to fruit flies that the business world will ever see." Indeed, nowhere in the history of business has there been an industry like disk drives, where changes in technology, market structure, global scope, and vertical integration have been so pervasive, rapid, and unrelenting. While this pace and complexity might be a nightmare for managers, my friend was right about its being fertile ground for research. Few industries offer researchers the same opportunities for developing theories about how different types of change cause certain types of firms to succeed or fail or for testing those theories as the industry repeats its cycles of change. This chapter summarizes the history of the disk drive industry in all its complexity. Some readers will be interested in it for the sake of history itself.1 But the value of understanding this history is that out of its complexity emerge a few stunningly simple and consistent factors that have repeatedly determined the success and failure of the industry's best firms. Simply put, when the best firms succeeded, they did so because they listened responsively to their customers and invested aggressively in the technology, products, and manufacturing capabilities that satisfied their customers' next-generation needs. But, paradoxically, when the best firms subsequently failed, it was for the same reasons—they listened responsively to their customers and invested aggressively in the technology, products, and manufacturing capabilities that satisfied their customers' next-generation needs. This is one of the innovator's dilemmas: Blindly following the maxim that good managers should keep close to their customers can sometimes be a fatal mistake. The history of the disk drive industry provides a framework for understanding when "keeping close to your customers" is good advice—and when it is not. The robustness of this framework could only be explored by researching the industry's history in careful detail. Some of that detail is recounted here, and elsewhere in this book, in the hope that readers who are immersed in the detail of their own industries will be better able to recognize how similar patterns have affected their own fortunes and those of their competitors. 21 HOW DISK DRIVES WORK Disk drives write and read information that computers use. They comprise read-write heads mounted at the end of an arm that swings over the surface of a rotating disk in much the same way that a phonograph needle and arm reach over a record; aluminum or glass disks coated with magnetic material; at least two electric motors, a spin motor that drives the rotation of the disks and an actuator motor that moves the head to the desired position over the disk; and a variety of electronic circuits that control the drive's operation and its interface with the computer. The read-write head is a tiny electromagnet whose polarity changes whenever the direction of the electrical current running through it changes. Because opposite magnetic poles attract, when the polarity of the head becomes positive, the polarity of the area on the disk beneath the head switches to negative, and vice versa. By rapidly changing the direction of current flowing through the head's electromagnet as the disk spins beneath the head, a sequence of positively and negatively oriented magnetic domains are created in concentric tracks on the disk's surface. Disk drives can use the positive and negative domains on the disk as a binary numeric system—1 and 0—to "write" information onto disks. Drives read information from disks in essentially the opposite process: Changes in the magnetic flux fields on the disk surface induce changes in the micro current flowing through the head. EMERGENCE OF THE EARLIEST DISK DRIVES A team of researchers at IBM's San Jose research laboratories developed the first disk drive between 1952 and 1956. Named RAMAC (for Random Access Method for Accounting and Control), this drive was the size of a large refrigerator, incorporated fifty twenty-four-inch disks, and could store 5 megabytes (MB) of information (see Figure 1.2). Most of the fundamental architectural concepts and component technologies that defined today's dominant disk drive design were also developed at IBM. These include its removable packs of rigid disks (introduced in 1961); the floppy disk drive (1971); and the Winchester architecture (1973). All had a powerful, defining influence on the way engineers in the rest of the industry defined what disk drives were and what they could do.

As IBM produced drives to meet its own needs, an independent disk drive industry emerged serving two distinct markets. A few firms developed the plug-compatible market (PCM) in the 1960s, selling souped-up copies of IBM drives directly to IBM customers at discount prices. Although most of IBM's competitors in computers (for example, Control Data, Burroughs, and Univac) were integrated vertically into the manufacture of their own disk drives, the emergence in the 1970s of smaller, nonintegrated computer makers such as Nixdorf, Wang, and Prime spawned an original equipment market (OEM) for disk drives as well. By 1976 about $1 billion worth of disk drives were produced, of which captive production accounted for 50 percent and PCM and OEM for about 25 percent each. The next dozen years unfolded a remarkable story of rapid growth, market turbulence, and technologydriven performance improvements. The value of drives produced rose to about $18 billion by 1995. By the mid-1980s the PCM market had become insignificant, while OEM output grew to represent about three-fourths of world production. Of the seventeen firms populating the industry in 1976—all of which were relatively large, diversified corporations such as Diablo, Ampex, Memorex, EMM, and Control Data—all except IBM's disk drive operation had failed or had been acquired by 1995. During this period an additional 129 firms entered the industry, and 109 of those also failed. Aside from IBM, Fujitsu, Hitachi, and NEC, all of the producers remaining by 1996 had entered the industry as start-ups after 1976. 23 Some have attributed the high mortality rate among the integrated firms that created the industry to its nearly unfathomable pace of technological change. Indeed, the pace of change has been breathtaking. The number of megabits (Mb) of information that the industry's engineers have been able to pack into a square inch of disk surface has increased by 35 percent per year, on average, from 50 Kb in 1967 to 1.7 Mb in 1973, 12 Mb in 1981, and 1100 Mb by 1995. The physical size of the drives was reduced at a similar pace: The smallest available 20 MB drive shrank from 800 cubic inches (in.3) in

1978 to 1.4 in.3 by 1993—a 35 percent annual rate of reduction. Figure 1.3 shows that the slope of the industry's experience curve (which correlates the cumulative number of terabytes (one thousand gigabytes) of disk storage capacity shipped in the industry's history to the constant-dollar price per megabyte of memory) was 53 percent—meaning that with each doubling of cumulative terabytes shipped, cost per megabyte fell to 53 percent of its former level. This is a much steeper rate of price decline than the 70 percent slope observed in the markets for most other microelectronics products. The price per megabyte has declined at about 5 percent per quarter for more than twenty years. THE IMPACT OF TECHNOLOGICAL CHANGE My investigation into why leading firms found it so difficult to stay atop the disk drive industry led me to develop the "technology mudslide hypothesis": Coping with the relentless onslaught of technology change was akin to trying to climb a mudslide raging down a hill. You have to scramble with everything you've got to stay on top of it, and if you ever once stop to catch your breath, you get buried.

Disk Drive Price Experience Curve

To test this hypothesis, I assembled and analyzed a database consisting of the technical and performance specifications of every model of disk drive introduced by every company in the world disk drive industry for each of the years between 1975 and 1994.2 This database enabled me to identify the firms that led in introducing each new technology; to trace how new technologies were diffused through the industry over time; to see which firms led and which lagged; and to measure the impact each technological innovation had on capacity, speed, and other parameters of disk drive performance. By carefully reconstructing the history of each technological change in the industry, the changes that catapulted entrants to success or that precipitated the failure of established leaders could be identified. This study led me to a very different view of technology change than the work of prior scholars on this question had led me to expect. Essentially, it revealed that neither the pace nor the difficulty of technological change lay at the root of the leading firms' failures. The technology mudslide hypothesis was wrong. The manufacturers of most products have established a trajectory of performance improvement over time.3 Intel, for example, pushed the speed of its microprocessors ahead by about 20 percent per year, from its 8 megahertz (MHz) 8088 processor in 1979 to its 133 MHz Pentium chip in 1994. Eli Lilly and Company improved the purity of its insulin from 50,000 impure parts per million (ppm) in 1925 to 10 ppm in 1980, a 14 percent annual rate of improvement. When a measurable trajectory of improvement has been established, determining whether a new technology is likely to improve a product's performance relative to earlier products is an unambiguous question. But in other cases, the impact of technological change is quite different. For instance, is a notebook computer better than a mainframe? This is an ambiguous question because the notebook computer established a completely new performance trajectory, with a definition of performance that differs substantially from the way mainframe performance is measured. Notebooks, as a consequence, are generally sold for very different uses. This study of technological change over the history of the disk drive industry revealed two types of technology change, each with very different effects on the industry's leaders. Technologies of the first sort sustained the industry's rate of improvement in product performance (total capacity and recording density were the two most common measures) and ranged in difficulty from incremental to radical. The industry's dominant firms always led in developing and adopting these technologies. By contrast, innovations of the second sort disrupted or redefined performance trajectories—and consistently resulted in the failure of the industry's leading firms.4 The remainder of this chapter illustrates the distinction between sustaining and disruptive technologies by describing prominent examples of each and summarizing the role these played in the industry's development. This discussion focuses on differences in how established firms came to lead or lag in developing and adopting new technologies, compared with entrant firms. To arrive at these examples, each new technology in the industry was examined. In analyzing which firms led and lagged at each of these points of change, I defined established firms to be those that had been established in the industry prior to the advent of the technology in question, practicing the prior technology. I defined entrant firms as those that were new to the industry at that point of technology change. Hence, a given firm would be considered an entrant at one specific point in the industry's history, for example, at the emergence of the 8-inch drive. Yet the same firm would be considered an established firm when technologies that emerged subsequent to the firm's entry were studied. 25 SUSTAINING TECHNOLOGICAL CHANGES In the history of the disk drive industry, most technology changes have sustained or reinforced established trajectories of product performance improvement. Figure 1.4, which compares the average recording density of drives that employed successive generations of head and disk technologies, maps an example of this. The first curve plots the density of drives that used conventional particulate oxide disk technology and ferrite head technology; the second charts the average density of drives that used new-technology thin-film heads and disks; the third marks the improvements in density achievable with the latest head technology, magneto-resistive heads.

Impact of New Read-Write Head Technologies in Sustaining the Trajectory of Improvement in Recording Density

The way such new technologies as these emerge to surpass the performance of the old resembles a series of intersecting technology S-curves.6 Movement along a given S-curve is generally the result of incremental improvements within an existing technological approach, whereas jumping onto the next technology curve implies adopting a radically new technology. In the cases measured in Figure 1.4, incremental advances, such as grinding the ferrite heads to finer, more precise dimensions and using smaller and more finely dispersed oxide particles on the disk's surface, led to the improvements in density from 1 to 20 megabits per square inch (Mbpsi) between 1976 and 1989. As S-curve theory would predict, the improvement in recording density obtainable with ferrite/oxide technology began to level off toward the end of the period, suggesting a maturing technology. The thin-film head and disk technologies' effect on the industry sustained performance improvement at its historical rate. Thin-film heads were barely established in the early 1990s, when even more advanced magneto-resistive head technology emerged. The impact of magneto-resistive technology sustained, or even accelerated, the rate of performance improvement.

a sustaining technological change of a very different character: an innovation in product architecture, in which the 14-inch Winchester drive is substituted for removable disk packs, which had been the dominant design between 1962 and 1978. Just as in the thin-film for ferrite/oxide substitution, the impact of Winchester technology sustained the historically established rate of performance improvement. Similar graphs could be constructed for most other technological innovations in the industry, such as embedded servo systems, RLL and PRML recording codes, higher RPM motors, and embedded interfaces. Some of these were straightforward technology improvements; others were radical departures. But all had a similar impact on the industry: They helped manufacturers to sustain the rate of historical performance improvement that their customers had come to expect.7 In literally every case of sustaining technology change in the disk drive industry, established firms led in development and commercialization. The emergence of new disk and head technologies illustrates this. In the 1970s, some manufacturers sensed that they were reaching the limit on the number of bits of information they could pack onto oxide disks. In response, disk drive manufacturers began studying ways of applying super-thin films of magnetic metal on aluminum to sustain the historical rate of improvements in recording density. The use of thin-film coatings was then highly developed in the integrated circuit industry, but its application to magnetic disks still presented substantial challenges. Experts estimate that the pioneers of thin-film disk technology—IBM, Control Data, Digital Equipment, Storage Technology, and Ampex—each took more than eight years and spent more than $50 million in that effort. Between 1984 and 1986, about two-thirds of the producers active in 1984 introduced drives with thin-film disks. The overwhelming majority of these were established industry incumbents. Only a few entrant firms attempted to use thin-film disks in their initial products, and most of those folded shortly after entry.

As was the case with thin-film disks, the introduction of thin-film heads entailed the sort of sustained investment that only established firms could handle. IBM and its rivals each spent more than $100 million developing thin-film heads. The pattern was repeated in the next-generation magneto-resistive head technology: The industry's largest firms—IBM, Seagate, and Quantum—led the race. The established firms were the leading innovators not just in developing risky, complex, and expensive component technologies such as thin-film heads and disks, but in literally every other one of the sustaining innovations in the industry's history. Even in relatively simple innovations, such as RLL recording codes (which took the industry from double- to triple-density disks), established firms were the successful pioneers, and entrant firms were the technology followers. This was also true for those architectural innovations—for example, 14-inch and 2.5-inch Winchester drives—whose impact was to sustain established improvement trajectories. Established firms beat out the entrants. Figure 1.6 summarizes this pattern of technology leadership among established and entrant firms offering products based on new sustaining technologies during the years when those technologies were emerging. The pattern is stunningly consistent. Whether the technology was radical or incremental, expensive or cheap, software or hardware, component or architecture, competence-enhancing or competence-destroying, the pattern was the same. When faced with sustaining technology change that gave existing customers something more and better in what they wanted, the leading practitioners of the prior technology led the industry in the development and adoption of the new. Clearly, the leaders in this industry did not fail because they became passive, arrogant, or risk-averse or because they couldn't keep up with the stunning rate of technological change. My technology mudslide hypothesis wasn't correct.

FAILURE IN THE FACE OF DISRUPTIVE TECHNOLOGICAL CHANGES Most technological change in the disk drive industry has consisted of sustaining innovations of the sort described above. In contrast, there have been only a few of the other sort of technological change, called disruptive technologies. These were the changes that toppled the industry's leaders. The most important disruptive technologies were the architectural innovations that shrunk the size of the drives—from 14-inch diameter disks to diameters of 8, 5.25, and 3.5-inches and then from 2.5 to 1.8 inches. Table 1.1 illustrates the ways these innovations were disruptive. Based on 1981 data, it compares the attributes of a typical 5.25-inch drive, a new architecture that had been in the market for less than a year, with those of a typical 8-inch drive, which at that time was the standard drive used by minicomputer manufacturers. Along the dimensions of performance important to established minicomputer manufacturers—capacity, cost per megabyte, and access time—the 8-inch product was vastly superior. The 5.25-inch architecture did not address the perceived needs of minicomputer manufacturers at that time. On the other hand, the 5.25-inch drive had features that appealed to the desktop personal computer market segment just emerging in the period between 1980 and 1982. It was small and lightweight, and, priced at around $2,000, it could be incorporated into desktop machines economically. Generally disruptive innovations were technologically straightforward, consisting of off-the-shelf components put together in a product architecture that was often simpler than prior approaches.8 They offered less of what customers in established markets wanted and so could rarely be initially employed there. They offered a different package of attributes valued only in emerging markets remote from, and unimportant to, the mainstream. 29 The trajectory map in Figure 1.7 shows how this series of simple but disruptive technologies proved to be the undoing of some very aggressive, astutely managed disk drive companies. Until the mid-1970s, 14-inch drives with removable packs of disks accounted for nearly all disk drive sales. The 14-inch Winchester architecture then emerged to sustain the trajectory of recording density improvement. Nearly all of these drives (removable disks and Winchesters) were sold to mainframe computer manufacturers, and the same companies that led the market in disk pack drives led the industry's transition to the Winchester technology. The trajectory map shows that the hard disk capacity provided in the median priced, typically configured mainframe computer system in 1974 was about 130 MB per computer. This increased at a 15 percent annual rate over the next fifteen years—a trajectory representing the disk capacity demanded by the typical users of new mainframe computers. At the same time, the capacity of the average 14-inch drive introduced for sale each year increased at a faster, 22 percent rate, reaching beyond the mainframe market to the large scientific and supercomputer markets.

2

Value Networks and the Impetus to Innovate

From the earliest studies of the problems of innovation, scholars, consultants, and managers have tried to explain why leading firms frequently stumble when confronting technology change. Most explanations either zero in on managerial, organizational, and cultural responses to technological change or focus on the ability of established firms to deal with radically new technology; doing the latter requires a very different set of skills from those that an established firm historically has developed. Both approaches, useful in explaining why some companies stumble in the face of technological change, are summarized below. The primary purpose of this chapter, however, is to propose a third theory of why good companies can fail, based upon the concept of a value network. The value network concept seems to have much greater power than the other two theories in explaining what we observed in the disk drive industry. ORGANIZATIONAL AND MANAGERIAL EXPLANATIONS OF FAILURE One explanation for why good companies fail points to organizational impediments as the source of the problem. While many analyses of this type stop with such simple rationales as bureaucracy, complacency, or "risk-averse" culture, some remarkably insightful studies exist in this tradition. Henderson and Clark,[1] for example, conclude that companies' organizational structures typically facilitate component-level innovations, because most product development organizations consist of subgroups that correspond to a product's components. Such systems work very well as long as the product's fundamental architecture does not require change. But, say the authors, when architectural technology change is required, this type of structure impedes innovations that require people and groups to communicate and work together in new ways. This notion has considerable face validity. In one incident recounted in Tracy Kidder's Pulitzer Prizewinning narrative, The Soul of a New Machine, Data General engineers developing a next-generation minicomputer intended to leapfrog the product position of Digital Equipment Corporation were allowed by a friend of one team member into his facility in the middle of the night to examine Digital's latest computer, which his company had just bought. When Tom West, Data General's project leader and a former long-time Digital employee, removed the cover of the DEC minicomputer and examined its structure, he saw "Digital's organization chart in the design of the product."2 Because an organization's structure and how its groups work together may have been established to facilitate the design of its dominant product, the direction of causality may ultimately reverse itself: The organization's structure and the way its groups learn to work together can then affect the way it can and cannot design new products. CAPABILITIES AND RADICAL TECHNOLOGY AS AN EXPLANATION 39 In assessing blame for the failure of good companies, the distinction is sometimes made between innovations requiring very different technological capabilities, that is, so-called radical change, and those that build upon well-practiced technological capabilities, often called incremental innovations.3 The notion is that the magnitude of the technological change relative to the companies' capabilities will determine which firms triumph after a technology invades an industry. Scholars who support this view find that established firms tend to be good at improving what they have long been good at doing, and that entrant firms seem better suited for exploiting radically new technologies, often because they import the technology into one industry from another, where they had already developed and practiced it. Clark, for example, has reasoned that companies build the technological capabilities in a product such as an automobile hierarchically and experientially.4 An organization's historical choices about which technological problems it would solve and which it would avoid determine the sorts of skills and knowledge it accumulates. When optimal resolution of a product or process performance problem demands a very different set of knowledge than a firm has accumulated, it may very well stumble. The research of Tushman, Anderson, and their associates supports Clark's hypothesis.5 They found that firms failed when a technological change destroyed the value of competencies previously cultivated and succeeded when new technologies enhanced them. The factors identified by these scholars undoubtedly affect the fortunes of firms confronted with new technologies. Yet the disk drive industry displays a series of anomalies accounted for by neither set of theories. Industry leaders first introduced sustaining technologies of every sort, including architectural and component innovations that rendered prior competencies irrelevant and made massive investments in skills and assets obsolete. Nevertheless, these same firms stumbled over technologically straightforward but disruptive changes such as the 8-inch drive. The history of the disk drive industry, indeed, gives a very different meaning to what constitutes a radical innovation among leading, established firms. As we saw, the nature of the technology involved (components versus architecture and incremental versus radical), the magnitude of the risk, and the time horizon over which the risks needed to be taken had little relationship to the patterns of leadership and followership observed. Rather, if their customers needed an innovation, the leading firms somehow mustered the resources and wherewithal to develop and adopt it. Conversely, if their customers did not want or need an innovation, these firms found it impossible to commercialize even technologically simple innovations. VALUE NETWORKS AND NEW PERSPECTIVE ON THE DRIVERS OF FAILURE What, then, does account for the success and failure of entrant and established firms? The following discussion synthesizes from the history of the disk drive industry a new perspective on the relation between success or failure and changes in technology and market structure. The concept of the value network—the context within which a firm identifies and responds to customers' needs, solves problems, procures input, reacts to competitors, and strives for profit—is central to this synthesis.6 Within a value network, each firm's competitive strategy, and particularly its past choices of markets, determines its perceptions of the economic value of a new technology. These perceptions, in turn, shape the rewards different firms expect to obtain through pursuit of sustaining and disruptive innovations.7 In established firms, expected rewards, in their turn, drive the allocation of resources 40 toward sustaining innovations and away from disruptive ones. This pattern of resource allocation accounts for established firms' consistent leadership in the former and their dismal performance in the latter. Value Networks Mirror Product Architecture Companies are embedded in value networks because their products generally are embedded, or nested hierarchically, as components within other products and eventually within end systems of use.8 Consider a 1980s-vintage management information system (MIS) for a large organization, as illustrated in Figure 2.1. The architecture of the MIS ties together various components—a mainframe computer; peripherals such as line printers and tape and disk drives; software; a large, air-conditioned room with cables running under a raised floor; and so on. At the next level, the mainframe computer is itself an architected system, comprising such components as a central processing unit, multi-chip packages and circuit boards, RAM circuits, terminals, controllers, and disk drives. Telescoping down still further, the disk drive is a system whose components include a motor, actuator, spindle, disks, heads, and controller. In turn, the disk itself can be analyzed as a system composed of an aluminum platter, magnetic material, adhesives, abrasives, lubricants, and coatings. Although the goods and services constituting such a system of use may all be produced within a single, extensively integrated corporation such as AT&T or IBM, most are tradable, especially in more mature markets. This means that, while Figure 2.1 is drawn to describe the nested physical architecture of a product system, it also implies the existence of a nested network of producers and markets through which the components at each level are made and sold to integrators at the next higher level in the system. Firms that design and assemble disk drives, for example, such as Quantum and Maxtor, procure read-write heads from firms specializing in the manufacture of those heads, and they buy disks from other firms and spin motors, actuator motors, and integrated circuitry from still others. At the next higher level, firms that design and assemble computers may buy their integrated circuits, terminals, disk drives, IC packaging, and power supplies from various firms that manufacture those particular products. This nested commercial system is a value network.

Metrics of Value The way value is measured differs across networks.9 In fact, the unique rank-ordering of the importance of various product performance attributes defines, in part, the boundaries of a value network.value network exhibits a very different rank-ordering of important product attributes, even for the same product. In the top-most value network, disk drive performance is measured in terms of capacity, speed, and reliability, whereas in the portable computing value network, the important performance attributes are ruggedness, low power consumption, and small size. Consequently, parallel value networks, each built around a different definition of what makes a product valuable, may exist within the same broadly defined industry.

structure. Research, engineering, and development costs are substantial. Manufacturing overheads are high relative to direct costs because of low unit volumes and customized product configurations. Selling directly to end users involves significant sales force costs, and the field service network to support the complicated machines represents a substantial ongoing expense. All these costs must be incurred in order to provide the types of products and services customers in this value network require. For these reasons, makers of mainframe computers, and makers of the 14-inch disk drives sold to them, historically needed gross profit margins of between 50 percent and 60 percent to cover the overhead cost structure inherent to the value network in which they competed. Competing in the portable computer value network, however, entails a very different cost structure. These computer makers incur little expense researching component technologies, preferring to build their machines with proven component technologies procured from vendors. Manufacturing involves assembling millions of standard products in low-labor-cost regions. Most sales are made through national retail chains or by mail order. As a result, companies in this value network can be profitable with gross margins of 15 percent to 20 percent. Hence, just as a value network is characterized by a specific rank-ordering of product attributes valued by customers, it is also characterized by a specific cost structure required to provide the valued products and services. Each value network's unique cost structure. Gross margins typically obtained by manufacturers of 14-inch disk drives, about 60 percent, are similar to those required by mainframe computer makers: 56 percent. Likewise, the margins 8-inch drive makers earned were similar to those earned by minicomputer companies (about 40 percent), and the margins typical of the desktop value network, 25 percent, also typified both the computer makers and their disk drive suppliers. The cost structures characteristic of each value network can have a powerful effect on the sorts of innovations firms deem profitable. Essentially, innovations that are valued within a firm's value network, or in a network where characteristic gross margins are higher, will be perceived as profitable. Those technologies whose attributes make them valuable only in networks with lower gross margins, on the other hand, will not be viewed as profitable, and are unlikely to attract resources or managerial interest. (We will explore the impact of each value network's characteristic cost structures upon the established firms' mobility and fortunes.

In sum, the attractiveness of a technological opportunity and the degree of difficulty a producer will encounter in exploiting it are determined by, among other factors, the firm's position in the relevant value network. As we shall see, the manifest strength of established firms in sustaining innovation and their weakness in disruptive innovation—and the opposite manifest strengths and weaknesses of entrant firms—are consequences not of differences in technological or organizational capabilities between incumbent and entrant firms, but of their positions in the industry's different value networks. TECHNOLOGY S-CURVES AND VALUE NETWORKS The technology S-curve forms the centerpiece of thinking about technology strategy. It suggests that the magnitude of a product's performance improvement in a given time period or due to a given amount of engineering effort is likely to differ as technologies mature. The theory posits that in the early stages of a technology, the rate of progress in performance will be relatively slow. As the technology becomes better understood, controlled, and diffused, the rate of technological improvement will accelerate.12 But in its mature stages, the technology will asymptotically approach a natural or physical limit such that ever greater periods of time or inputs of engineering effort will be required to achieve improvements. Figure 2.5 illustrates the resulting pattern. Many scholars have asserted that the essence of strategic technology management is to identify when the point of inflection on the present technology's S-curve has been passed, and to identify and develop whatever successor technology rising from below will eventually supplant the present approach. Hence, as depicted by the dotted curve in Figure 2.5, the challenge is to successfully switch technologies at the point where S-curves of old and new intersect. The inability to anticipate new technologies threatening from below and to switch to them in a timely way has often been cited as the cause of failure of established firms and as the source of advantage for entrant or attacking firms.

MANAGERIAL DECISION MAKING AND DISRUPTIVE TECHNOLOGICAL CHANGE Competition within the value networks in which companies are embedded defines in many ways how the firms can earn their money. The network defines the customers' problems to be addressed by the firm's products and services and how much can be paid for solving them. Competition and customer demands in the value network in many ways shape the firms' cost structure, the firm size required to remain competitive, and the necessary rate of growth. Thus, managerial decisions that make sense for companies outside a value network may make no sense at all for those within it, and vice versa. We saw, in chapter 1, a stunningly consistent pattern of successful implementation of sustaining innovations by established firms and their failure to deal with disruptive ones. The pattern was consistent because the managerial decisions that led to those outcomes made sense. Good managers do what makes sense, and what makes sense is primarily shaped by their value network. This decision-making pattern, outlined in the six steps below, emerged from my interviews with more than eighty managers who played key roles in the disk drive industry's leading firms, both incumbents and entrants, at times when disruptive technologies had emerged. In these interviews I tried to reconstruct, as accurately and from as many points of view as possible, the forces that influenced these 48 firms' decision-making processes regarding the development and commercialization of technologies either relevant or irrelevant to the value networks in which the firms were at the time embedded. My findings consistently showed that established firms confronted with disruptive technology change did not have trouble developing the requisite technology: Prototypes of the new drives had often been developed before management was asked to make a decision. Rather, disruptive projects stalled when it came to allocating scarce resources among competing product and technology development proposals (allocating resources between the two value networks shown at right and left in Figure 2.6, for example). Sustaining projects addressing the needs of the firms' most powerful customers (the new waves of technology within the value network depicted in Figure 2.5) almost always preempted resources from disruptive technologies with small markets and poorly defined customer needs. This characteristic pattern of decisions is summarized in the following pages. Because the experience was so archetypical, the struggle of Seagate Technology, the industry's dominant maker of 5.25-inch drives, to successfully commercialize the disruptive 3.5-inch drive is recounted in detail to illustrate each of the steps in the pattern.15 Step 1: Disruptive Technologies Were First Developed within Established Firms Although entrants led in commercializing disruptive technologies, their development was often the work of engineers at established firms, using bootlegged resources. Rarely initiated by senior management, these architecturally innovative designs almost always employed off-the-shelf components. Thus, engineers at Seagate Technology, the leading 5.25-inch drive maker, were, in 1985, the second in the industry to develop working prototypes of 3.5-inch models. They made some eighty prototype models before the issue of formal project approval was raised with senior management. The same thing happened earlier at Control Data and Memorex, the dominant 14-inch drive makers, where engineers had designed working 8-inch drives internally, nearly two years before the product appeared in the market. Step 2: Marketing Personnel Then Sought Reactions from Their Lead Customers The engineers then showed their prototypes to marketing personnel, asking whether a market for the smaller, less expensive (and lower performance) drives existed. The marketing organization, using its habitual procedure for testing the market appeal of new drives, showed the prototypes to lead customers of the existing product line, asking them for an evaluation.16 Thus, Seagate marketers tested the new 3.5-inch drives with IBM's PC Division and other makers of XT- and AT-class desktop personal computers—even though the drives had significantly less capacity than the mainstream desktop market demanded. Not surprisingly, therefore, IBM showed no interest in Seagate's disruptive 3.5-inch drives. IBM's engineers and marketers were looking for 40 and 60 MB drives, and they already had a slot for 5.25- inch drives designed into their computer; they needed new drives that would take them further along their established performance trajectory. Finding little customer interest, Seagate's marketers drew up pessimistic sales forecasts. In addition, because the products were simpler, with lower performance, forecast profit margins were lower than those for higher performance products, and Seagate's financial 49 analysts, therefore, joined their marketing colleagues in opposing the disruptive program. Working from such input, senior managers shelved the 3.5-inch drive—just as it was becoming firmly established in the laptop market. This was a complex decision, made in a context of competing proposals to expend the same resources to develop new products that marketers felt were critical to remaining competitive with current customers and achieving aggressive growth and profit targets. "We needed a new model," recalled a former Seagate manager, "which could become the next ST412 [a very successful product generating $300 million sales annually in the desktop market that was near the end of its life cycle]. Our forecasts for the 3.5-inch drive were under $50 million because the laptop market was just emerging, and the 3.5- inch product just didn't fit the bill." Seagate managers made an explicit decision not to pursue the disruptive technology. In other cases, managers did approve resources for pursuing a disruptive product—but, in the day-to-day decisions about how time and money would actually be allocated, engineers and marketers, acting in the best interests of the company, consciously and unconsciously starved the disruptive project of resources necessary for a timely launch. When engineers at Control Data, the leading 14-inch drive maker, were officially chartered to develop CDC's initial 8-inch drives, its customers were looking for an average of 300 MB per computer, whereas CDC's earliest 8-inch drives offered less than 60 MB. The 8-inch project was given low priority, and engineers assigned to its development kept getting pulled off to work on problems with 14-inch drives being designed for more important customers. Similar problems plagued the belated launches of Quantum's and Micropolis's 5.25-inch products. Step 3: Established Firms Step Up the Pace of Sustaining Technological Development In response to the needs of current customers, the marketing managers threw impetus behind alternative sustaining projects, such as incorporating better heads or developing new recording codes. These gave customers what they wanted and could be targeted at large markets to generate the necessary sales and profits for maintaining growth. Although often involving greater development expense, such sustaining investments appeared far less risky than investments in the disruptive technology: The customers existed, and their needs were known. Seagate's decision to shelve the 3.5-inch drive in 1985 to 1986, for example, seems starkly rational. Its view downmarket (in terms of the disk drive trajectory map) was toward a small total market forecast for 1987 for 3.5-inch drives. Gross margins in that market were uncertain, but manufacturing executives predicted that costs per megabyte for 3.5-inch drives would be much higher than for 5.25- inch drives. Seagate's view upmarket was quite different. Volumes in 5.25-inch drives with capacities of 60 to 100 MB were forecast to be $500 million by 1987. Companies serving the 60 to 100 MB market were earning gross margins of between 35 and 40 percent, whereas Seagate's margins in its high-volume 20 MB drives were between 25 and 30 percent. It simply did not make sense for Seagate to put its resources behind the 3.5-inch drive when competing proposals to move upmarket by developing its ST251 line of drives were also being actively evaluated. After Seagate executives shelved the 3.5-inch project, the firm began introducing new 5.25-inch models at a dramatically accelerated rate. In 1985, 1986, and 1987, the numbers of new models 50 annually introduced as a percentage of the total number of its models on the market in the prior year were 57, 78, and 115 percent, respectively. And during the same period, Seagate incorporated complex and sophisticated new component technologies such as thin-film disks, voice-coil actuators,17 RLL codes, and embedded SCSI interfaces. Clearly, the motivation in doing this was to win the competitive wars against other established firms, which were making similar improvements, rather than to prepare for an attack by entrants from below.18 Step 4: New Companies Were Formed, and Markets for the Disruptive Technologies Were Found by Trial and Error New companies, usually including frustrated engineers from established firms, were formed to exploit the disruptive product architecture. The founders of the leading 3.5-inch drive maker, Conner Peripherals, were disaffected employees from Seagate and Miniscribe, the two largest 5.25-inch manufacturers. The founders of 8-inch drive maker Micropolis came from Pertec, a 14-inch drive manufacturer, and the founders of Shugart and Quantum defected from Memorex.19 The start-ups, however, were as unsuccessful as their former employers in attracting established computer makers to the disruptive architecture. Consequently, they had to find new customers. The applications that emerged in this very uncertain, probing process were the minicomputer, the desktop personal computer, and the laptop computer. In retrospect, these were obvious markets for hard drives, but at the time, their ultimate size and significance were highly uncertain. Micropolis was founded before the emergence of the desk-side minicomputer and word processor markets in which its products came to be used. Seagate began when personal computers were simple toys for hobbyists, two years before IBM introduced its PC. And Conner Peripherals got its start before Compaq knew the potential size of the portable computer market. The founders of these firms sold their products without a clear marketing strategy—essentially selling to whoever would buy. Out of what was largely a trial-and-error approach to the market, the ultimately dominant applications for their products emerged. Step 5: The Entrants Moved Upmarket Once the start-ups had discovered an operating base in new markets, they realized that, by adopting sustaining improvements in new component technologies,20 they could increase the capacity of their drives at a faster rate than their new market required. They blazed trajectories of 50 percent annual improvement, fixing their sights on the large, established computer markets immediately above them on the performance scale. The established firms' views downmarket and the entrant firms' views upmarket were asymmetrical. In contrast to the unattractive margins and market size that established firms saw when eyeing the new, emerging markets for simpler drives, the entrants saw the potential volumes and margins in the upscale, high-performance markets above them as highly attractive. Customers in these established markets eventually embraced the new architectures they had rejected earlier, because once their needs for capacity and speed were met, the new drives' smaller size and architectural simplicity made them cheaper, faster, and more reliable than the older architectures. Thus, Seagate, which started in the desktop personal computer market, subsequently invaded and came to dominate the minicomputer, 51 engineering workstation, and mainframe computer markets for disk drives. Seagate, in turn, was driven from the desktop personal computer market for disk drives by Conner and Quantum, the pioneering manufacturers of 3.5-inch drives. Step 6: Established Firms Belatedly Jumped on the Bandwagon to Defend Their Customer Base When the smaller models began to invade established market segments, the drive makers that had initially controlled those markets took their prototypes off the shelf (where they had been put in Step 3) and introduced them in order to defend their customer base in their own market. By this time, of course, the new architecture had shed its disruptive character and become fully performancecompetitive with the larger drives in the established markets. Although some established manufacturers were able to defend their market positions through belated introduction of the new architecture, many found that the entrant firms had developed insurmountable advantages in manufacturing cost and design experience, and they eventually withdrew from the market. The firms attacking from value networks below brought with them cost structures set to achieve profitability at lower gross margins. The attackers therefore were able to price their products profitably, while the defending, established firms experienced a severe price war. For established manufacturers that did succeed in introducing the new architectures, survival was the only reward. None ever won a significant share of the new market; the new drives simply cannibalized sales of older products to existing customers. Thus, as of 1991, almost none of Seagate's 3.5-inch drives had been sold to portable/laptop manufacturers: Its 3.5-inch customers still were desktop computer manufacturers, and many of its 3.5-inch drives continued to be shipped with frames permitting them to be mounted in XT- and AT-class computers designed to accommodate 5.25-inch drives. Control Data, the 14-inch leader, never captured even a 1 percent share of the minicomputer market. It introduced its 8-inch drives nearly three years after the pioneering start-ups did, and nearly all of its drives were sold to its existing mainframe customers. Miniscribe, Quantum, and

Micropolis all had the same cannibalistic experience when they belatedly introduced disruptive technology drives. They failed to capture a significant share of the new market, and at best succeeded in defending a portion of their prior business. The popular slogan "stay close to your customers" appears not always to be robust advice.21 One instead might expect customers to lead their suppliers toward sustaining innovations and to provide no leadership—or even to explicitly mislead—in instances of disruptive technology change.22 FLASH MEMORY AND THE VALUE NETWORK The predictive power of the value network framework is currently being tested with the emergence of flash memory: a solid-state semiconductor memory technology that stores data on silicon memory chips. Flash differs from conventional dynamic random access memory (DRAM) technology in that the chip retains the data even when the power is off. Flash memory is a disruptive technology. Flash chips consume less than 5 percent of the power that a disk drive of equivalent capacity would consume, and 52 because they have no moving parts, they are far more rugged than disk memory. Flash chips have disadvantages, of course. Depending on the amount of memory, the cost per megabyte of flash can be between five and fifty times greater than disk memory. And flash chips are not as robust for writing: They can only be overwritten a few hundred thousand times before wearing out, rather than a few million times for disk drives. The initial applications for flash memory were in value networks quite distant from computing; they were in devices such as cellular phones, heart monitoring devices, modems, and industrial robots in which individually packaged flash chips were embedded. Disk drives were too big, too fragile, and used too much power to be used in these markets. By 1994, these applications for individually packaged flash chips—"socket flash" in industry parlance—accounted for $1.3 billion in industry revenues, having grown from nothing in 1987. In the early 1990s, the flash makers produced a new product format, called a flash card: credit cardsized devices on which multiple flash chips, linked and governed by controller circuitry, were mounted. The chips on flash cards were controlled by the same control circuitry, SCSI (Small Computer Standard Interface, an acronym first used by Apple), as was used in disk drives, meaning that in concept, a flash card could be used like a disk drive for mass storage. The flash card market grew from $45 million in 1993 to $80 million in 1994, and forecasters were eyeing a $230 million flash card market by 1996. Will flash cards invade the disk drive makers' core markets and supplant magnetic memory? If they do, what will happen to the disk drive makers? Will they stay atop their markets, catching this new technological wave? Or will they be driven out?

IMPLICATIONS OF THE VALUE NETWORK FRAMEWORK FOR INNOVATION Value networks strongly define and delimit what companies within them can and cannot do. This chapter closes with five propositions about the nature of technological change and the problems successful incumbent firms encounter, which the value network perspective highlights. 1. The context, or value network, in which a firm competes has a profound influence on its ability to marshal and focus the necessary resources and capabilities to overcome the technological and organizational hurdles that impede innovation. The boundaries of a value network are determined by a unique definition of product performance—a rank-ordering of the importance of various performance attributes differing markedly from that employed in other systems-of-use in a broadly defined industry. Value networks are also defined by particular cost structures inherent in addressing customers' needs within the network. 2. A key determinant of the probability of an innovative effort's commercial success is the degree to which it addresses the well-understood needs of known actors within the value network. Incumbent firms are likely to lead their industries in innovations of all sorts—architecture and components—that address needs within their value network, regardless of intrinsic technological character or difficulty. These are straightforward innovations; their value and application are clear. Conversely, incumbent firms are likely to lag in the development of technologies—even those in which the technology involved is intrinsically simple—that only address customers' needs in emerging value networks. Disruptive innovations are complex because their value and application are uncertain, according to the criteria used by incumbent firms. 3. Established firms' decisions to ignore technologies that do not address their customers' needs become fatal when two distinct trajectories interact. The first defines the performance demanded over time within a given value network, and the second traces the performance that technologists are able to provide within a given technological paradigm. The trajectory of performance improvement that technology is able to provide may have a distinctly different slope from the trajectory of performance improvement demanded in the system-of-use by downstream customers within any given value network. When the slopes of these two trajectories are similar, we expect the technology to remain relatively contained within its initial value network. But when the slopes differ, new technologies that are initially performance-competitive only within emerging or commercially remote value networks may migrate into other networks, providing a vehicle for innovators in new networks to attack established ones. When such an attack occurs, it is because technological progress has diminished the relevancce of differences in the rank-ordering of performance attributes across different value networks. For example, the disk drive attributes of size and weight were far more important in the desktop computing value network than they were in the mainframe and minicomputer value networks. When technological progress in 5.25-inch drives enabled manufacturers to satisfy the attribute prioritization in the mainframe and minicomputer networks, which prized total capacity and high speed, as well as that in the desktop network, the boundaries between the value networks ceased to be barriers to entry for 5.25-inch drive makers. 4. Entrant firms have an attacker's advantage over established firms in those innovations—generally new product architectures involving little new technology per se—that disrupt or redefine the level, rate, and direction of progress in an established technological trajectory. This is so because such technologies generate no value within the established network. The only way established firms can lead 57 in commercializing such technologies is to enter the value network in which they create value. As Richard Tedlow noted in his history of retailing in America (in which supermarkets and discount retailing play the role of disruptive technologies), "the most formidable barrier the established firms faced is that they did not want to do this."25 5. In these instances, although this "attacker's advantage" is associated with a disruptive technology change, the essence of the attacker's advantage is in the ease with which entrants, relative to incumbents, can identify and make strategic commitments to attack and develop emerging market applications, or value networks. At its core, therefore, the issue may be the relative flexibility of successful established firms versus entrant firms to change strategies and cost structures, not technologies. These propositions provide new dimensions for analyzing technological innovation. In addition to the required capabilities inherent in new technologies and in the innovating organization, firms faced with disruptive technologies must examine the implications of innovation for their relevant value networks. The key considerations are whether the performance attributes implicit in the innovation will be valued within the networks already served by the innovator; whether other networks must be addressed or new ones created in order to realize value for the innovation; and whether market and technological trajectories may eventually intersect, carrying technologies that do not address customers' needs today to squarely address their needs in the future.

3

Disruptive Technological Change in the Mechanical Excavator Industry

Excavators and their steam shovel predecessors are huge pieces of capital equipment sold to excavation contractors. While few observers consider this a fast-moving, technologically dynamic industry, it has points in common with the disk drive industry: Over its history, leading firms have successfully adopted a series of sustaining innovations, both incremental and radical, in components and architecture, but almost the entire population of mechanical shovel manufacturers was wiped out by a disruptive technology—hydraulics—that the leaders' customers and their economic structure had caused them initially to ignore. Although in disk drives such invasions of established markets occurred within a few years of the initial emergence of each disruptive technology, the triumph of hydraulic excavators took twenty years. Yet the disruptive invasion proved just as decisive and difficult to counter in excavators as those in the disk drive industry.1 LEADERSHIP IN SUSTAINING TECHNOLOGICAL CHANGE From William Smith Otis' invention of the steam shovel in 1837 through the early 1920s, mechanical earthmoving equipment was steam-powered. A central boiler sent steam through pipes to small steam engines at each point where power was required in the machine. Through a system of pulleys, drums, and cables, these engines manipulated frontward-scooping buckets, as illustrated in Figure 3.1. Originally, steam shovels were mounted on rails and used to excavate earth in railway and canal construction. American excavator manufacturers were tightly clustered in northern Ohio and near Milwaukee.

In the early 1920s, when there were more than thirty-two steam shovel manufacturers based in the United States, the industry faced a major technological upheaval, as gasoline-powered engines were substituted for steam power.2 This transition to gasoline power falls into the category that Henderson and Clark label radical technological transition. The fundamental technological concept in a key component (the engine) changed from steam to internal combustion, and the basic architecture of the product changed. Where steam shovels used steam pressure to power a set of steam engines to extend and retract the cables that actuated their buckets, gasoline shovels used a single engine and a very different system of gearing, clutches, drums, and brakes to wind and unwind the cable. Despite the radical nature of the technological change, however, gasoline technology had a sustaining impact on the mechanical excavator industry. Gasoline engines were powerful enough to enable contractors to move earth faster, more reliably, and at lower cost than any but the very largest steam shovels. The leading innovators in gasoline engine technology were the industry's dominant firms, such as Bucyrus, Thew, and Marion. Twenty-three of the twenty-five largest makers of steam shovels successfully negotiated the transition to gasoline power. As there were a few entrant firms among the gasoline technology leaders in the 1920s, but the established firms dominated this transition. Beginning in about 1928, the established manufacturers of gasoline-powered shovels initiated the next major, but less radical, sustaining technological transition—to shovels powered by diesel engines and electric motors. A further transition, made after World War II, introduced the arched boom design, which allowed longer reach, bigger buckets, and better down-reaching flexibility. The established firms continued to embrace and succeed with each of these innovations.

Excavation contractors themselves actually pioneered a number of other important sustaining innovations, first modifying their own equipment in the field to make it perform better and then manufacturing excavators incorporating those features to sell to the broader market.4 THE IMPACT OF DISRUPTIVE HYDRAULICS TECHNOLOGY The next major technological change precipitated widespread failure in the industry. Beginning shortly after World War II and continuing through the late 1960s, while the dominant source of power remained the diesel engine, a new mechanism emerged for extending and lifting the bucket: hydraulically actuated systems replaced the cable-actuated systems. Only four of the thirty or so established manufacturers of cable-actuated equipment in business in the 1950s (Insley, Koehring, Little Giant, and Link Belt) had successfully transformed themselves into sustainable hydraulic excavator manufacturers by the 1970s. A few others survived by withdrawing into making such equipment as huge, cable-actuated draglines for strip mining and dredging.5 Most of the others failed. The firms that overran the excavation equipment industry at this point were all entrants into the hydraulics generation: J. I. Case, John Deere, Drott, Ford, J. C. Bamford, Poclain, International Harvester, Caterpillar, O & K, Demag, Leibherr, Komatsu, and Hitachi.6 Why did this happen? Performance Demanded in the Mechanical Excavator Market Excavators are one of many types of earthmoving equipment. Some equipment, such as bulldozers, loaders, graders, and scrapers, essentially push, smooth, and lift earth. Excavators7 have been used to dig holes and trenches, primarily in three markets: first and largest, the general excavation market, composed of contractors who dig holes for basements or civil engineering projects such as canal construction; second, sewer and piping contractors, who generally dig long trenches; and third, open pit or strip mining. In each of these markets, contractors have tended to measure the functionality of 63 mechanical excavators by their reach or extension distance and by the cubic yards of earth lifted in a single scoop.8 In 1945, sewer and piping contractors used machines whose bucket capacity averaged about 1 cubic yard (best for digging relatively narrow trenches), while the average general excavation contractor used excavators that hefted 2 1/2 cubic yards per scoop and mining contractors used shovels holding about 5 cubic yards. The average bucket capacity used in each of these markets increased at about 4 percent per year, a rate of increase constrained by other factors in the broader system-of-use. The logistical problems of transporting large machines into and out of typical construction sites, for example, helped limit the rate of increase demanded by contractors. The Emergence and Trajectory of Improvement of Hydraulic Excavation The first hydraulic excavator was developed by a British company, J. C. Bamford, in 1947. Similar products then emerged simultaneously in several American companies in the late 1940s, among them, the Henry Company, of Topeka, Kansas, and Sherman Products, Inc., of Royal Oak, Michigan. The approach was labeled "Hydraulically Operated Power Take-Off," yielding an acronym that became the name of the third entrant to hydraulic excavating in the late 1940s, HOPTO.9 Their machines were called backhoes because they were mounted on the back of industrial or farm tractors. Backhoes excavated by extending the shovel out, pushing it down into the earth,10 curling or articulating the shovel under the slice of earth, and lifting it up out of the hole. Limited by the power and strength of available hydraulic pumps' seals, the capacity of these early machines was a mere 1/4 cubic yard, as graphed in Figure 3.3. Their reach was also limited to about six feet. Whereas the best cable excavators could rotate a full 360 degrees on their track base, the most flexible backhoes could rotate only 180 degrees.

Because their capacity was so small and their reach so short, hydraulic excavators were of no use to mining, general excavation, or sewer contractors, who were demanding machines with buckets that held 1 to 4 cubic yards. As a result, the entrant firms had to develop a new application for their products. They began to sell their excavators as attachments for the back of small industrial and farm tractors made by Ford, J. I. Case, John Deere, International Harvester, and Massey Ferguson. Small residential contractors purchased these units to dig narrow ditches from water and sewer lines in the street to the foundations of houses under construction. These very small jobs had never warranted the expense or time required to bring in a big, imprecise, cable-actuated, track-driven shovel, so the trenches had always been dug by hand. Hydraulic backhoes attached to highly mobile tractors could do these jobs in less than an hour per house, and they became extremely popular with contractors building large tract subdivisions during the housing booms that followed World War II and the Korean War. These early backhoes were sold through tractor and implement dealerships accustomed to dealing with small customers. The early users of hydraulic excavators were, in a word, very different from the mainstream customers of the cable shovel manufacturers—in size, in needs, and in the distribution channels through which they bought. They constituted a new value network for mechanical excavation. Interestingly, just as the performance of smaller-architecture disk drives was measured in different metrics than the performance of large drives (weight, ruggedness, and power consumption versus capacity and speed), the performance of the first backhoes was measured differently from the performance of cable-actuated equipment. The metrics featured most prominently in early product literature of hydraulic backhoes were shovel width (contractors wanted to dig narrow, shallow trenches) and the speed and maneuverability of the tractor.

excerpted from an early product brochure from Sherman Products for its "Bobcat" hydraulic backhoe, illustrates this. Sherman called its Bobcat a "digger," showed it operating in tight quarters, and claimed it could travel over sod with minimum damage. The Bobcat was mounted on a Ford tractor. (Ford subsequently acquired the Sherman Bobcat line.) The featured attributes, of course, were simply irrelevant to contractors whose bread was buttered by big earthmoving projects. These differences in the rank-ordering of performance attributes defined the boundaries of the industry's value networks.

THE RESPONSE TO HYDRAULICS BY THE ESTABLISHED EXCAVATOR MANUFACTURERS Just as Seagate Technology was one of the first firms to develop prototype 3.5-inch drives, Bucyrus Erie, the leading cable shovel maker, was keenly aware of the emergence of hydraulic excavating technology. By 1950 (about two years after the first backhoe appeared) Bucyrus purchased a fledgling hydraulic backhoe company, the Milwaukee Hydraulics Corporation. Bucyrus faced precisely the same problem in marketing its hydraulic backhoe as Seagate had faced with its 3.5-inch drives: Its most powerful mainstream customers had no use for it. Bucyrus Erie's response was a new product, introduced in 1951, called the "Hydrohoe." Instead of using three hydraulic cylinders, it used only two, one to curl the shovel into the earth and one to "crowd" or draw the shovel toward the cab; it used a cable mechanism to lift the shovel. The Hydrohoe 66 was thus a hybrid of the two technologies, reminiscent of the early transoceanic steamships outfitted with sails.11 There is no evidence, however, that the Hydrohoe's hybrid design resulted from Bucyrus engineers' being "stuck" in some sort of cable-based engineering paradigm. Rather, the cable lift mechanism was the only viable way at that time, based on the state of hydraulics technology, to give the Hydrohoe the bucket capacity and reach that Bucyrus marketers thought they needed to appeal to their existing customers' needs. Figure 3.5 presents an excerpt from an early Hydrohoe product brochure. Note the differences from Sherman's marketing approach: Bucyrus labeled the Hydrohoe a "dragshovel," showed it in an open field, and claimed it could "get a heaping load on every pass"—all intended to appeal to general excavation contractors. Rather than commercialize the disruptive technology in the value network in which the current attributes of hydraulics were prized, Bucyrus tried to adapt the technology to fit its own value network. Despite this attempt, the Hydrohoe was still too limited in capacity and reach and did not sell well to Bucyrus' customers. Bucyrus kept its Hydrohoe on the market for over a decade, attempting periodically to upgrade its performance to make it acceptable to its customers, but the machine was never commercially successful. Ultimately, the company returned to the cable shovels that its customers needed.

4

Give Responsibility for Disruptive Technologies

Most executives would like to believe that they're in charge of their organizations, that they make the crucial decisions and that when they decide that something should be done everyone snaps to and executes. This chapter expands on the view already introduced: that in practice, it is a company's customers who effectively control what it can and cannot do. As we have seen in the disk drive industry, companies were willing to bet enormous amounts on technologically risky projects when it was clear that their customers needed the resulting products. But they were unable to muster the wherewithal to execute much simpler disruptive projects if existing, profitable customers didn't need the products. This observation supports a somewhat controversial theory called resource dependence, propounded by a minority of management scholars,1 which posits that companies' freedom of action is limited to satisfying the needs of those entities outside the firm (customers and investors, primarily) that give it the resources it needs to survive. Drawing heavily upon concepts from biological evolution, resource dependence theorists assert that organizations will survive and prosper only if their staffs and systems serve the needs of customers and investors by providing them with the products, services, and profit they require. Organizations that do not will ultimately die off, starved of the revenues they need to survive.2 Hence, through this survival-of-the-fittest mechanism, those firms that rise to prominence in their industries generally will be those whose people and processes are most keenly tuned to giving their customers what they want. The controversy with this theory arises when its proponents conclude that managers are powerless to change the courses of their firms against the dictates of their customers. Even if a manager has a bold vision to take her or his company in a very different direction, the power of the customer-focused people and processes in any company well-adapted to survival in its competitive environment will reject the manager's attempts to change direction. Therefore, because they provide the resources upon which the firm is dependent, it is the customers, rather than the managers, who really determine what a firm will do. It is forces outside the organization, rather than the managers within it, that dictate the company's course. Resource dependence theorists conclude that the real role of managers in companies whose people and systems are well-adapted to survival is, therefore, only a symbolic one. For those of us who have managed companies, consulted for management, or taught future managers, this is a most disquieting thought. We are there to manage, to make a difference, to formulate and implement strategy, to accelerate growth and improve profits. Resource dependence violates our very reason for being. Nonetheless, the findings reported in this book provide rather stunning support for the theory of resource dependence—especially for the notion that the customer-focused resource allocation and decision-making processes of successful companies are far more powerful in directing investments than are executives' decisions. Clearly, customers wield enormous power in directing a firm's investments. What, then, should managers do when faced with a disruptive technology that the company's customers explicitly do not 90 want? One option is to convince everyone in the firm that the company should pursue it anyway, that it has long-term strategic importance despite rejection by the customers who pay the bills and despite lower profitability than the upmarket alternatives. The other option would be to create an independent organization and embed it among emerging customers that do need the technology. Which works best? Managers who choose the first option essentially are picking a fight with a powerful tendency of organizational nature—that customers, not managers, essentially control the investment patterns of a company. By contrast, managers who choose the second option align themselves with this tendency, harnessing rather than fighting its power. The cases presented in this chapter provide strong evidence that the second option offers far higher probabilities of success than the first. INNOVATION AND RESOURCE ALLOCATION The mechanism through which customers control the investments of a firm is the resource allocation process—the process that determines which initiatives get staff and money and which don't. Resource allocation and innovation are two sides of the same coin: Only those new product development projects that do get adequate funding, staffing, and management attention have a chance to succeed; those that are starved of resources will languish. Hence, the patterns of innovation in a company will mirror quite closely the patterns in which resources are allocated. Good resource allocation processes are designed to weed out proposals that customers don't want. When these decision-making processes work well, if customers don't want a product, it won't get funded; if they do want it, it will. This is how things must work in great companies. They must invest in things customers want—and the better they become at doing this, the more successful they will be. As we saw in chapter 4, resource allocation is not simply a matter of top-down decision making followed by implementation. Typically, senior managers are asked to decide whether to fund a project only after many others at lower levels in the organization have already decided which types of project proposals they want to package and send on to senior management for approval and which they don't think are worth the effort. Senior managers typically see only a well-screened subset of the innovative ideas generated.3 And even after senior management has endorsed funding for a particular project, it is rarely a "done deal." Many crucial resource allocation decisions are made after project approval—indeed, after product launch—by mid-level managers who set priorities when multiple projects and products compete for the time of the same people, equipment, and vendors. As management scholar Chester Barnard has noted: From the point of view of the relative importance of specific decisions, those of executives properly call for first attention. But from the point of view of aggregate importance, it is not decisions of executives, but of non-executive participants in organizations which should enlist major interest. [Italics added.]4 So how do non-executive participants make their resource allocation decisions? They decide which projects they will propose to senior management and which they will give priority to, based upon their understanding of what types of customers and products are most profitable to the company. Tightly coupled with this is their view of how their sponsorship of different proposals will affect their own 91 career trajectories within the company, a view that is formed heavily by their understanding of what customers want and what types of products the company needs to sell more of in order to be more profitable. Individuals' career trajectories can soar when they sponsor highly profitable innovation programs. It is through these mechanisms of seeking corporate profit and personal success, therefore, that customers exert a profound influence on the process of resource allocation, and hence on the patterns of innovation, in most companies. SUCCESS IN DISRUPTIVE DISK DRIVE TECHNOLOGY It is possible to break out of this system of customer control, however. Three cases in the history of the disk drive industry demonstrate how managers can develop strong market positions in a disruptive technology. In two cases, managers harnessed, rather than fought, the forces of resource dependence: They spun out independent companies to commercialize the disruptive technology. In the third, the manager chose to fight these forces, and survived the project, exhausted. Quantum and Plus Development As we have seen, Quantum Corporation, a leading maker of 8-inch drives sold in the minicomputer market in the early 1980s, completely missed the advent of 5.25-inch drives: It introduced its first versions nearly four years after those drives first appeared in the market. As the 5.25-inch pioneers began to invade the minicomputer market from below, for all the reasons already described, Quantum's sales began to sag. In 1984 several Quantum employees saw a potential market for a thin 3.5-inch drive plugged into an expansion slot in IBM XT- and AT-class desktop computers—drives that would be sold to personal computer users rather than the OEM minicomputer manufacturers that had accounted for all of Quantum's revenue. They determined to leave Quantum and start a new firm to commercialize their idea. Rather than let them leave unencumbered, however, Quantum's executives financed and retained 80 percent ownership of this spinoff venture, called Plus Development Corporation, and set the company up in different facilities. It was a completely self-sufficient organization, with its own executive staff and all of the functional capabilities required in an independent company. Plus was extremely successful. It designed and marketed its drives but had them manufactured under contract by Matsushita Kotobuki Electronics (MKE) in Japan. As sales of Quantum's line of 8-inch drives began to evaporate in the mid-1980s, they were offset by Plus's growing "Hardcard" revenues. By 1987, sales of Quantum's 8- and 5.25-inch products had largely disappeared. Quantum then purchased the remaining 20 percent of Plus, essentially closed down the old corporation, and installed Plus's executives in Quantum's most senior positions. They then reconfigured Plus's 3.5-inch products to appeal to OEM desktop computer makers, such as Apple, just as the capacity vector for 3.5-inch drives was invading the desktop market, as shown in the disk drive trajectory map in Figure 1.7. Quantum, thus reconstituted as a 3.5-inch drive maker, has aggressively adopted sustaining component technology innovations, moving upmarket toward 92 engineering workstations, and has also successfully negotiated the sustaining architectural innovation into 2.5-inch drives. By 1994 the new Quantum had become the largest unit-volume producer of disk drives in the world.

Control Data in Oklahoma Control Data Corporation (CDC) effected the same self-reconstitution—once. CDC was the dominant manufacturer of 14-inch drives sold into the OEM market between 1965 and 1982; its market share fluctuated between 55 and 62 percent. When the 8-inch architecture emerged in the late 1970s, however, CDC missed it—by three years. The company never captured more than a fraction of the 8- inch market, and those 8-inch drives that it did sell were sold almost exclusively to defend its established customer base of mainframe computer manufacturers. The reason was resources and managerial emphasis: Engineers and marketers at the company's principal Minneapolis facility kept getting pulled off the 8-inch program to resolve problems in the launch of next-generation 14-inch products for CDC's mainstream customers. CDC launched its first 5.25-inch model two years after Seagate's pioneering product appeared in 1980. This time, however, CDC located its 5.25-inch effort in Oklahoma City. This was done, according to one manager, "not to escape CDC's Minneapolis engineering culture, but to isolate the [5.25-inch product] group from the company's mainstream customers." Although it was late in the market and never regained its former dominant position, CDC's foray into 5.25-inch drives was profitable, and at times the firm commanded a 20 percent share of higher-capacity 5.25-inch drives. Micropolis: Transition by Managerial Force Micropolis Corporation, an early disk drive leader founded in 1978 to make 8-inch drives, was the only other industry player to successfully make the transition to a disruptive platform. It did not use the spinout strategy that had worked for Quantum and Control Data, however, choosing instead to manage the change from within the mainstream company. But even this exception supports the rule that customers exert exceptionally powerful influence over the investments that firms can undertake successfully. Micropolis began to change in 1982, when founder and CEO Stuart Mabon intuitively perceived the trajectories of market demand and technology supply mapped in Figure 1.7 and decided that the firm should become primarily a maker of 5.25-inch drives. While initially hoping to keep adequate resources focused on developing its next generation of 8-inch drives so that Micropolis could straddle both markets,6 he assigned the company's premier engineers to the 5.25-inch program. Mabon recalls that it took "100 percent of my time and energy for eighteen months" to keep adequate resources focused on the 5.25-inch program, because the organization's own mechanisms allocated resources to where the customers were—8-inch drives. By 1984, Micropolis had failed to keep pace with competition in the minicomputer market for disk drives and withdrew its remaining 8-inch models. With Herculean effort, however, it did succeed in its 5.25-inch programs. Figure 5.1 shows why this struggle occurred: In making the transition, Micropolis assumed a position on a very different technological trajectory. It had to walk away from every one of 93 its major customers and replace the lost revenues with sales of the new product line to an entirely different group of desktop computer makers. Mabon remembers the experience as the most exhausting of his life. Micropolis finally introduced a 3.5-inch product in 1993. That was the point at which the product had progressed to pack more than 1 gigabyte in the 3.5-inch platform. At that level, Micropolis could sell the 3.5-inch drive to its existing customers.

The struggles recounted earlier of Seagate Technology's attempts to sell 3.5-inch drives and of Bucyrus Erie's failed attempt to sell its early Hydrohoe only to its mainstream customers illustrate how the theory of resource dependence can be applied to cases of disruptive technologies. In both instances, Seagate and Bucyrus were among the first in their industries to develop these disruptive products. But despite senior managers' decisions to introduce them, the impetus or organizational energy required to launch the products aggressively into the appropriate value networks simply did not coalesce—until customers needed them. Should we then accept the corollary stipulated by resource-dependence theorists that managers are merely powerless individuals? Hardly. In the Introduction, exploring the image of how people learned to fly, I noted that all attempts had ended in failure as long as they consisted of fighting fundamental laws of nature. But once laws such as gravity, Bernoulli's principle, and the notions of lift, drag and resistance began to be understood, and flying machines were designed that accounted for or harnessed 94 those laws, people flew quite successfully. By analogy, this is what Quantum and Control Data did. By embedding independent organizations within an entirely different value network, where they were dependent upon the appropriate set of customers for survival, those managers harnessed the powerful forces of resource dependence. The CEO of Micropolis fought them, but he won a rare and costly victory. Disruptive technologies have had deadly impact in many industries besides disk drives, mechanical excavators, and steel.7 The following pages summarize the effect of disruptive technologies in three other industries—computers, retailing, and printers—to highlight how the only companies in those industries that established strong market positions in the disruptive technologies were those which, like Quantum and Control Data, harnessed rather than fought the forces of resource dependence.

Similarly, none of the makers of minicomputers became a significant factor in the desktop personal computer market, because to them the desktop computer was a disruptive technology. The PC market was created by another set of entrants, including Apple, Commodore, Tandy, and IBM. The minicomputer makers were exceptionally prosperous and highly regarded by investors, the business press, and students of good management—until the late 1980s, when the technological trajectory of the desktop computer intersected with the performance demanded by those who had previously bought minicomputers. The missile-like attack of the desktop computer from below severely wounded every minicomputer maker. Several of them failed. None established a viable position in the desktop personal computer value network. A similar sequence of events characterized the emergence of the portable computer, where the market was created and dominated by a set of entrants like Toshiba, Sharp, and Zenith. Apple and IBM, the leading desktop makers, did not introduce portable models until the portables' performance trajectory intersected with the computing needs of their customers. Probably none of these firms has been so deeply wounded by disruptive technology as Digital Equipment. DEC fell from fortune to folly in just a few years, as stand-alone workstations and networked desktop computers obviated most customers' needs for minicomputers almost overnight. 95 DEC didn't stumble for lack of trying, of course. Four times between 1983 and 1995 it introduced lines of personal computers targeted at consumers, products that were technologically much simpler than DEC's minicomputers. But four times it failed to build businesses in this value network that were perceived within the company as profitable. Four times it withdrew from the personal computer market. Why? DEC launched all four forays from within the mainstream company.8 For all of the reasons so far recounted, even though executive-level decisions lay behind the move into the PC business, those who made the day-to-day resource allocation decisions in the company never saw the sense in investing the necessary money, time, and energy in low-margin products that their customers didn't want. Higherperformance initiatives that promised upscale margins, such as DEC's super-fast Alpha microprocessor and its adventure into mainframe computers, captured the resources instead. In trying to enter the desktop personal computing business from within its mainstream organization, DEC was forced to straddle the two different cost structures intrinsic to two different value networks. It simply couldn't hack away enough overhead cost to be competitive in low-end personal computers because it needed those costs to remain competitive in its higher-performance products. Yet IBM's success in the first five years of the personal computing industry stands in stark contrast to the failure of the other leading mainframe and minicomputer makers to catch the disruptive desktop computing wave. How did IBM do it? It created an autonomous organization in Florida, far away from its New York state headquarters, that was free to procure components from any source, to sell through its own channels, and to forge a cost structure appropriate to the technological and competitive requirements of the personal computing market. The organization was free to succeed along metrics of success that were relevant to the personal computing market. In fact, some have argued that IBM's subsequent decision to link its personal computer division much more closely to its mainstream organization was an important factor in IBM's difficulties in maintaining its profitability and market share in the personal computer industry. It seems to be very difficult to manage the peaceful, unambiguous coexistence of two cost structures, and two models for how to make money, within a single company. The conclusion that a single organization might simply be incapable of competently pursuing disruptive technology, while remaining competitive in mainstream markets, bothers some "can-do" managers—and, in fact, most managers try to do exactly what Micropolis and DEC did: maintain their competitive intensity in the mainstream, while simultaneously trying to pursue disruptive technology. The evidence is strong that such efforts rarely succeed; position in one market will suffer unless two separate organizations, embedded within the appropriate value networks, pursue their separate customers. KRESGE, WOOLWORTH, AND DISCOUNT RETAILING In few industries has the impact of disruptive technology been felt so pervasively as in retailing, where discounters seized dominance from traditional department and variety stores. The technology of discount retailing was disruptive to traditional operations because the quality of service and selection offered by discounters played havoc with the accustomed metrics of quality retailing. Moreover, the cost structure required to compete profitably in discount retailing was fundamentally different than that which department stores had developed to compete within their value networks. 96 The first discount store was Korvette's, which began operating a number of outlets in New York in the mid-1950s. Korvette's and its imitators operated at the very low end of retailing's product line, selling nationally known brands of standard hard goods at 20 to 40 percent below department store prices. They focused on products that "sold themselves" because customers already knew how to use them. Relying on national brand image to establish the value and quality of their products, these discounters eliminated the need for knowledgeable salespeople; they also focused on the group of customers least attractive to mainstream retailers: "young wives of blue collar workers with young children."9 This was counter to the upscale formulas department stores historically had used to define quality retailing and to improve profits. Discounters didn't accept lower profits than those of traditional retailers, however; they just earned their profits through a different formula. In the simplest terms, retailers cover their costs through the gross margin, or markup, they charge over the cost of the merchandise they sell. Traditional department stores historically marked merchandise up by 40 percent and turned their inventory over four times in a year—that is, they earned 40 percent on the amount they invested in inventory, four times during the year, for a total return on inventory investment of 160 percent. Variety stores earned somewhat lower profits through a formula similar to that used by the department stores. Discount retailers earned a return on inventory investment similar to that of department stores, but through a different model: low gross margins and high inventory turns.

The history of discount retailing vividly recalls the history of minimill steel making. Just like the minimills, discounters took advantage of their cost structure to move upmarket and seize share from competing traditional retailers at a stunning rate: first at the low end, in brand-name hard goods such as hardware, small appliances, and luggage, and later in territory further to the northeast such as home furnishings and clothing. Figure 5.2 illustrates how stunning the discounters' invasion was: Their share of retailing revenues in the categories of goods they sold rose from 10 percent in 1960 to nearly 40 percent a scant six years later.

Just as in disk drives and excavators, a few of the leading traditional retailers—notably S. S. Kresge, F. W. Woolworth, and Dayton Hudson—saw the disruptive approach coming and invested early. None of the other major retail chains, including Sears, Montgomery Ward, J. C. Penney, and R. H. Macy, made a significant attempt to create a business in discount retailing. Kresge (with its Kmart chain) and Dayton Hudson (with the Target chain) succeeded.10 They both created focused discount retailing organizations that were independent from their traditional business. They recognized and harnessed the forces of resource dependence. By contrast, Woolworth failed in its venture (Woolco), trying to launch it from within the F. W. Woolworth variety store company. A detailed comparison of the approaches of Kresge and Woolworth, which started from very similar positions, lends additional insight into why establishing independent organizations to pursue disruptive technology seems to be a necessary condition for success. S. S. Kresge, then the world's second largest variety store chain, began studying discount retailing in 1957, while discounting was still in its infancy. By 1961, both Kresge and its rival F. W. Woolworth (the world's largest variety store operator) had announced initiatives to enter discount retailing. Both firms opened stores in 1962, within three months of each other. The performance of the Woolco and Kmart ventures they launched, however, subsequently differed dramatically. A decade later, Kmart's sales approached $3.5 billion while Woolco's sales were languishing unprofitably at $0.9 billion.11 In making its commitment to discount retailing, Kresge decided to exit the variety store business entirely: In 1959 it hired a new CEO, Harry Cunningham, whose sole mission was to convert Kresge into a discounting powerhouse. Cunningham, in turn, brought in an entirely new management team, so that by 1961 there "was not a single operating vice president, regional manager, assistant regional manager, or regional merchandise manager who was not new on the job."12 In 1961 Cunningham stopped opening any new variety stores, embarking instead on a program of closing about 10 percent of Kresge's existing variety operations each year. This represented a wholesale refocusing of the company on discount retailing. Woolworth, on the other hand, attempted to support a program of sustaining improvements in technology, capacity, and facilities in its core variety store businesses while simultaneously investing in disruptive discounting. The managers charged with improving the performance of Woolworth's variety stores were also charged with building "the largest chain of discount houses in America." CEO Robert Kirkwood asserted that Woolco "would not conflict with the company's plans for growth and 98 expansion in the regular variety store operations," and that no existing stores would be converted to a discount format.13 Indeed, as discount retailing hit its most frenzied expansion phase in the 1960s, Woolworth was opening new variety stores at the pace it had set in the 1950s. Unfortunately (but predictably), Woolworth proved unable to sustain within a single organization the two different cultures, and two different models of how to make a profit, that were required to be successful in variety and discount retailing. By 1967 it had dropped the term "discount" from all Woolco advertising, adopting the term "promotional department store" instead. Although initially Woolworth had set up a separate administrative staff for its Woolco operation, by 1971 more rational, cost-conscious heads had prevailed. In a move designed to increase sales per square foot in both Woolco and Woolworth divisions, the two subsidiaries have been consolidated operationally on a regional basis. Company officials say the consolidation—which involves buying offices, distribution facilities and management personnel at the regional level—will help both to develop better merchandise and more efficient stores. Woolco will gain the benefits of Woolworth's buying resources, distribution facilities and additional expertise in developing specialty departments. In return, Woolworth will gain Woolco's knowhow in locating, designing, promoting and operating large stores over 100,000 sq. ft.14 What was the impact of this cost-saving consolidation? It provided more evidence that two models for how to make money cannot peacefully coexist within a single organization. Within a year of this consolidation, Woolco had increased its markups such that its gross margins were the highest in the discount industry—about 33 percent. In the process, its inventory turns fell from the 7x it originally had achieved to 4x. The formula for profit that had long sustained F. W. Woolworth (35 percent margins for four inventory turns or 140 percent return on inventory investment) was ultimately demanded of Woolco as well.

Woolworth's organizational strategy for succeeding in disruptive discount retailing was the same as Digital Equipment's strategy for launching its personal computer business. Both founded new ventures within the mainstream organization that had to earn money by mainstream rules, and neither could achieve the cost structure and profit model required to succeed in the mainstream value network. SURVIVAL BY SUICIDE: HEWLETT-PACKARD'S LASER JET AND INK-JET PRINTERS Hewlett-Packard's experience in the personal computer printer business illustrates how a company's pursuit of a disruptive technology by spinning out an independent organization might entail, in the end, killing another of its business units. Hewlett-Packard's storied success in manufacturing printers for personal computers becomes even more remarkable when one considers its management of the emergence of bubble-jet or ink-jet technology. Beginning in the mid-1980s, HP began building a huge and successful business around laser jet printing technology. The laser jet was a discontinuous improvement over dot-matrix printing, the previously dominant personal computer printing technology, and HP built a commanding market lead. When an alternative way of translating digital signals into images on paper (ink-jet technology) first appeared, there were vigorous debates about whether laser jet or ink jet would emerge as the dominant design in personal printing. Experts lined up on both sides of the question, offering HP extensive advice on which technology would ultimately become the printer of choice on the world's desktops.15 Although it was never framed as such in the debates of the time, ink-jet printing was a disruptive technology. It was slower than the laser jet, its resolution was worse, and its cost per printed page was higher. But the printer itself was smaller and potentially much less expensive than the laser jet. At these lower prices, it promised lower gross margin dollars per unit than the laser jet. Thus, the ink-jet printer was a classic disruptive product, relative to the laser jet business. Rather than place its bet exclusively with one or the other, and rather than attempt to commercialize the disruptive ink-jet from within the existing printer division in Boise, Idaho, HP created a completely autonomous organizational unit, located in Vancouver, Washington, with responsibility for making the ink-jet printer a success. It then let the two businesses compete against each other. Each has behaved classically. As shown in Figure 5.4, the laser jet division has moved sharply upmarket, in a strategy reminiscent of 14-inch drives, mainframe computers, and integrated steel mills. HP's laser jet printers can print at high speeds with exceptional resolution; handle hundreds of fonts and complicated graphics; print on two sides of the page; and serve multiple users on a network. They have also gotten larger physically. The ink-jet printer isn't as good as the laser jet and may never be. But the critical question is whether the ink jet could ever be as good a printer as the personal desktop computing market demands. The answer appears to be yes. The resolution and speed of ink-jet printers, while still inferior to those of laser jets, are now clearly good enough for many students, professionals, and other un-networked users of desktop computers. HP's ink-jet printer business is now capturing many of those who would formerly have been laser jet users. Ultimately, the number of users at the highest-performance end of the market, toward which the 100 laser jet division is headed, will probably become small. One of HP's businesses may, in the end, have killed another. But had HP not set up its ink-jet business as a separate organization, the ink-jet technology would probably have languished within the mainstream laser jet business, leaving one of the other companies now actively competing in the ink-jet printer business, such as Canon, as a serious threat to HP's printer business. And by staying in the laser business, as well, HP has joined IBM's mainframe business and the integrated steel companies in making a lot of money while executing an upmarket retreat.

5

Match the Size of the Organization to the Size of the Market

Managers who confront disruptive technological change must be leaders, not followers, in commercializing disruptive technologies. Doing so requires implanting the projects that are to develop such technologies in commercial organizations that match in size the market they are to address. These assertions are based on two key findings of this study: that leadership is more crucial in coping with disruptive technologies than with sustaining ones, and that small, emerging markets cannot solve the near-term growth and profit requirements of large companies. The evidence from the disk drive industry shows that creating new markets is significantly less risky and more rewarding than entering established markets against entrenched competition. But as companies become larger and more successful, it becomes even more difficult to enter emerging markets early enough. Because growing companies need to add increasingly large chunks of new revenue each year just to maintain their desired rate of growth, it becomes less and less possible that small markets can be viable as vehicles through which to find these chunks of revenue. As we shall see, the most straightforward way of confronting this difficulty is to implant projects aimed at commercializing disruptive technologies in organizations small enough to get excited about smallmarket opportunities, and to do so on a regular basis even while the mainstream company is growing. ARE THE PIONEERS REALLY THE ONES WITH ARROWS IN THEIR BACKS? A crucial strategic decision in the management of innovation is whether it is important to be a leader or acceptable to be a follower. Volumes have been written on first-mover advantages, and an offsetting amount on the wisdom of waiting until the innovation's major risks have been resolved by the pioneering firms. "You can always tell who the pioneers were," an old management adage goes. "They're the ones with the arrows in their backs." As with most disagreements in management theory, neither position is always right. Indeed, some findings from the study of the disk drive industry give some insight into when leadership is critical and when followership makes better sense. Leadership in Sustaining Technologies May Not Be Essential One of the watershed technologies affecting the pace at which disk drive makers have increased the recording density of their drives was the thin-film read/write head. We saw in chapter 1 that despite the radically different, competence-destroying character of the technology, the $100 million and five-to- 103 fifteen year expense of developing it, the firms that led in this technology were the leading, established disk drive manufacturers. Because of the risk involved in the technology's development and its potential importance to the industry, the trade press began speculating in the late 1970s about which competitor would lead with thin-film heads. How far might conventional ferrite head technology be pushed? Would any drive makers get squeezed out of the industry race because they placed a late or wrong bet on the new head technology? Yet, it turned out, whether a firm led or followed in this innovation did not make a substantial difference in its competitive position. This is illustrated in Figures 6.1 and 6.2. Figure 6.1 shows when each of the leading firms introduced its first model employing thin-film head technology. The vertical axis measures the recording density of the drive. The bottom end of the line for each firm denotes the maximum recording density it had achieved before it introduced a model with a thin-film head. The top end of each line indicates the density of the first model each company introduced with a thin-film head. Notice the wide disparity in the points at which the firms felt it was important to introduce the new technology. IBM led the industry, introducing its new head when it had achieved 3 megabits (Mb) per square inch. Memorex and Storage Technology similarly took a leadership posture with respect to this technology. At the other end, Fujitsu and Hitachi pushed the performance of conventional ferrite heads nearly ten times beyond the point where IBM first introduced the technology, choosing to be followers, rather than leaders, in thin-film technology.

What benefit, if any, did leadership in this technology give to the pioneers? There is no evidence that the leaders gained any significant competitive advantage over the followers; none of the firms that pioneered thin-film technology gained significant market share on that account. In addition, pioneering firms appear not to have developed any sort of learning advantage enabling them to leverage their early lead to attain higher levels of density than did followers. Evidence of this is displayed in Figure 6.2. The horizontal axis shows the order in which the firms adopted thin-film heads. Hence, IBM was the first, Memorex, the second, and Fujitsu the fifteenth. The vertical axis gives the rank ordering of the recording density of the most advanced model marketed by each firm in 1989. If the early adopters of thin-film heads enjoyed some sort of experience-based advantage over the late adopters, then we would expect the points in the chart to slope generally from the upper left toward the lower right. The chart shows instead that there is no relationship between leadership and followership in thin-film heads and any subsequent technological edge.1 Each of the other sustaining technologies in the industry's history present a similar picture. There is no evidence that any of the leaders in developing and adopting sustaining technologies developed a discernible competitive advantage over the followers.

Leadership in Disruptive Technologies Creates Enormous Value

In contrast to the evidence that leadership in sustaining technologies has historically conferred little advantage on the pioneering disk drive firms, there is strong evidence that leadership in disruptive technology has been very important. The companies that entered the new value networks enabled by disruptive generations of disk drives within the first two years after those drives appeared were six times more likely to succeed than those that entered later. Eighty-three companies entered the U.S. disk drive industry between 1976 and 1993. Thirty-five of these were diversified concerns, such as Memorex, Ampex, 3M, and Xerox, that made other computer peripheral equipment or other magnetic recording products. Forty-eight were independent startup companies, many being financed by venture capital and headed by people who previously had worked for other firms in the industry. These numbers represent the complete census of all firms that ever were incorporated and/or were known to have announced the design of a hard drive, whether or not they actually sold any. It is not a statistical sample of firms that might be biased in favor or against any type of firm.

Each quadrant displays the number of companies that entered using the strategy represented. Under the S (for "success") are the number of firms that successfully generated $100 million in revenues in at least one year, even if the firm subsequently failed; F (for "failure") shows the number of firms that failed ever to reach the $100 million revenue threshold and that have subsequently exited the industry; N (for "no") indicates the number of firms for which there is as yet no verdict because, while still operating in 1994, they had not yet reached $100 million in sales; and T (for "total") lists the total number of firms that entered in each category.5 The column labeled "% Success" indicates the percentage of the total number of firms that reached $100 million in sales. Finally, beneath the matrix are the sums of the data in the two quadrants above. The numbers beneath the matrix show that only three of the fifty-one firms (6 percent) that entered established markets ever reached the $100 million revenue benchmark. In contrast, 37 percent of the firms that led in disruptive technological innovation—those entering markets that were less than two years old—surpassed the $100 million level, as shown on the right side of Table 6.1. Whether a firm 107 was a start-up or a diversified firm had little impact on its success rate. What mattered appears not to have been its organizational form, but whether it was a leader in introducing disruptive products and creating the markets in which they were sold.6 Only 13 percent of the firms that entered attempting to lead in sustaining component technologies (the top half of the matrix) succeeded, while 20 percent of the firms that followed were successful. Clearly, the lower-right quadrant offered the most fertile ground for success. The cumulative sales numbers in the right-most columns in each quadrant show the total, cumulative revenues logged by all firms pursuing each of the strategies; these are summarized below the matrix. The result is quite stunning. The firms that led in launching disruptive products together logged a cumulative total of $62 billion dollars in revenues between 1976 and 1994.7 Those that followed into the markets later, after those markets had become established, logged only $3.3 billion in total revenue. It is, indeed, an innovator's dilemma. Firms that sought growth by entering small, emerging markets logged twenty times the revenues of the firms pursuing growth in larger markets. The difference in revenues per firm is even more striking: The firms that followed late into the markets enabled by disruptive technology, on the left half of the matrix, generated an average cumulative total of $64.5 million per firm. The average company that led in disruptive technology generated $1.9 billion in revenues. The firms on the left side seem to have made a sour bargain. They exchanged a market risk, the risk that an emerging market for the disruptive technology might not develop after all, for a competitive risk, the risk of entering markets against entrenched competition.8 COMPANY SIZE AND LEADERSHIP IN DISRUPTIVE TECHNOLOGIES Despite evidence that leadership in disruptive innovation pays such huge dividends, established firms, as shown in the first four chapters of this book, often fail to take the lead. Customers of established firms can hold the organizations captive, working through rational, well-functioning resource allocation processes to keep them from commercializing disruptive technologies. One cruel additional disabling factor that afflicts established firms as they work to maintain their growth rate is that the larger and more successful they become, the more difficult it is to muster the rationale for entering an emerging market in its early stages, when the evidence above shows that entry is so crucial. Good managers are driven to keep their organizations growing for many reasons. One is that growth rates have a strong effect on share prices. To the extent that a company's stock price represents the discounted present value of some consensus forecast of its future earnings stream, then the level of the stock price—whether it goes up or down—is driven by changes in the projected rate of growth in earnings.9 In other words, if a company's current share price is predicated on a consensus growth forecast of 20 percent, and the market's consensus for growth is subsequently revised downward to 15 percent growth, then the company's share price will likely fall—even though its revenues and earnings will still be growing at a healthy rate. A strong and increasing stock price, of course, gives a company access to capital on favorable terms; happy investors are a great asset to a company. Rising share prices make stock option plans an inexpensive way to provide incentive to and to reward valuable employees. When share prices stagnate or fall, options lose their value. In addition, company growth creates room at the top for high-performing employees to expand the scope of their responsibilities. When companies stop growing, they begin losing many of their most promising future leaders, who see less opportunity for advancement. 108 Finally, there is substantial evidence that growing companies find it much easier to justify investments in new product and process technologies than do companies whose growth has stopped.10 Unfortunately, companies that become large and successful find that maintaining growth becomes progressively more difficult. The math is simple: A $40 million company that needs to grow profitably at 20 percent to sustain its stock price and organizational vitality needs an additional $8 million in revenues the first year, $9.6 million the following year, and so on; a $400 million company with a 20 percent targeted growth rate needs new business worth $80 million in the first year, $96 million in the next, and so on; and a $4 billion company with a 20 percent goal needs to find $800 million, $960 million, and so on, in each successive year. This problem is particularly vexing for big companies confronting disruptive technologies. Disruptive technologies facilitate the emergence of new markets, and there are no $800 million emerging markets. But it is precisely when emerging markets are small—when they are least attractive to large companies in search of big chunks of new revenue—that entry into them is so critical. How can a manager of a large, successful company deal with these realities of size and growth when confronted by disruptive change? I have observed three approaches in my study of this problem: 1. Try to affect the growth rate of the emerging market, so that it becomes big enough, fast enough, to make a meaningful dent on the trajectory of profit and revenue growth of a large company. 2. Wait until the market has emerged and become better defined, and then enter after it "has become large enough to be interesting." 3. Place responsibility to commercialize disruptive technologies in organizations small enough that their performance will be meaningfully affected by the revenues, profits, and small orders flowing from the disruptive business in its earliest years. As the following case studies show, the first two approaches are fraught with problems. The third has its share of drawbacks too, but offers more evidence of promise. CASE STUDY: PUSHING THE GROWTH RATE OF AN EMERGING MARKET The history of Apple Computer's early entry into the hand-held computer, or personal digital assistant (PDA), market helps to clarify the difficulties confronting large companies in small markets. Apple Computer introduced its Apple I in 1976. It was at best a preliminary product with limited functionality, and the company sold a total of 200 units at $666 each before withdrawing it from the market. But the Apple I wasn't a financial disaster. Apple had spent modestly on its development, and both Apple and its customers learned a lot about how desktop personal computers might be used. Apple incorporated this learning into its Apple II computer, introduced in 1977, which was highly successful. Apple sold 43,000 Apple II computers in the first two years they were on the market,11 and the product's success positioned the company as the leader in the personal computer industry. On the basis of the Apple II's success Apple went public in 1980. 109 A decade after the release of the

Apple II, Apple Computer had grown into a $5 billion company, and like all large and successful companies, it found itself having to add large chunks of revenue each year to preserve its equity value and organizational vitality. In the early 1990s, the emerging market for hand-held PDAs presented itself as a potential vehicle for achieving that needed growth. In many ways, this opportunity, analogous to that in 1978 when the Apple II computer helped shape its industry, was a great fit for Apple. Apple's distinctive design expertise was in user-friendly products, and userfriendliness and convenience were the basis of the PDA concept. How did Apple approach this opportunity? Aggressively. It invested scores of millions of dollars to develop its product, dubbed the "Newton." The Newton's features were defined through one of the most thoroughly executed market research efforts in corporate history; focus groups and surveys of every type were used to determine what features consumers would want. The PDA had many of the characteristics of a disruptive computing technology, and recognizing the potential problems, Apple CEO John Sculley made the Newton's development a personal priority, promoting the product widely, and ensuring that the effort got the technical and financial resources it needed. Apple sold 140,000 Newtons in 1993 and 1994, its first two years on the market. Most observers, of course, viewed the Newton as a big flop. Technically, its handwriting recognition capabilities were disappointing, and its wireless communications technologies had made it expensive. But what was most damning was that while Sculley had publicly positioned the Newton as a key product to sustain the company's growth, its first-year sales amounted to about 1 percent of Apple's revenues. Despite all the effort, the Newton made hardly a dent in Apple's need for new growth. But was the Newton a failure? The timing of Newton's entry into the handheld market was akin to the timing of the Apple II into the desktop market. It was a market-creating, disruptive product targeted at an undefinable set of users whose needs were unknown to either themselves or Apple. On that basis, Newton's sales should have been a pleasant surprise to Apple's executives: It outsold the Apple II in its first two years by a factor of more than three to one. But while selling 43,000 units was viewed as an IPO-qualifying triumph in the smaller Apple of 1979, selling 140,000 Newtons was viewed as a failure in the giant Apple of 1994. As chapter 7 will show, disruptive technologies often enable something to be done that previously had been deemed impossible. Because of this, when they initially emerge, neither manufacturers nor customers know how or why the products will be used, and hence do not know what specific features of the product will and will not ultimately be valued. Building such markets entails a process of mutual discovery by customers and manufacturers—and this simply takes time. In Apple's development of the desktop computer, for example, the Apple I failed, the first Apple II was lackluster, and the Apple II+ succeeded. The Apple III was a market failure because of quality problems, and the Lisa was a failure. The first two generations of the Macintosh computer also stumbled. It wasn't until the third iteration of the Macintosh that Apple and its customers finally found "it": the standard for convenient, userfriendly computing to which the rest of the industry ultimately had to conform.12 In launching the Newton, however, Apple was desperate to short-circuit this coalescent process for defining the ultimate product and market. It assumed that its customers knew what they wanted and spent very aggressively to find out what this was. (As the next chapter will show, this is impossible.) Then to give customers what they thought they wanted, Apple had to assume the precarious role of a sustaining technology leader in an emerging industry. It spent enormous sums to push mobile data communications and handwriting recognition technologies beyond the state of the art. And finally, it spent aggressively to convince people to buy what it had designed. 110 Because emerging markets are small by definition, the organizations competing in them must be able to become profitable at small scale. This is crucial because organizations or projects that are perceived as being profitable and successful can continue to attract financial and human resources both from their corporate parents and from capital markets. Initiatives perceived as failures have a difficult time attracting either. Unfortunately, the scale of the investments Apple made in its Newton in order to hasten the emergence of the PDA market made it very difficult to earn an attractive return. Hence, the Newton came to be broadly viewed as a flop. As with most business disappointments, hindsight reveals the faults in Apple's Newton project. But I believe that the root cause of Apple's struggle was not inappropriate management. The executives' actions were a symptom of a deeper problem: Small markets cannot satisfy the near-term growth requirements of big organizations. CASE STUDY: WAITING UNTIL A MARKET IS LARGE ENOUGH TO BE INTERESTING A second way that many large companies have responded to the disruptive technology trap is to wait for emerging markets to "get large enough to be interesting" before they enter. Sometimes this works, as IBM's well-timed 1981 entry into the desktop PC business demonstrated. But it is a seductive logic that can backfire, because the firms creating new markets often forge capabilities that are closely attuned to the requirements of those markets and that later entrants find difficult to replicate. Two examples from the disk drive industry illustrate this problem. Priam Corporation, which ascended to leadership of the market for 8-inch drives sold to minicomputer makers after its entry in 1978, had built the capability in that market to develop its drives on a two-year rhythm. This pace of new product introduction was consistent with the rhythm by which its customers, minicomputer makers, introduced their new products into the market. Seagate's first 5.25-inch drive, introduced to the emerging desktop market in 1980, was disruptively slow compared to the performance of Priam's drives in the minicomputer market. But by 1983, Seagate and the other firms that led in implementing the disruptive 5.25-inch technology had developed a oneyear product introduction rhythm in their market. Because Seagate and Priam achieved similar percentage improvements in speed with each new product generation, Seagate, by introducing new generations on a one-year rhythm, quickly began to converge on Priam's performance advantage. Priam introduced its first 5.25-inch drive in 1982. But the rhythm by which it introduced its subsequent 5.25-inch models was the two-year capability it had honed in the minicomputer market—not the oneyear cycle required to compete in the desktop marketplace. As a consequence, it was never able to secure a single major OEM order from a desktop computer manufacturer: It just couldn't hit their design windows with its new products. And Seagate, by taking many more steps forward than did Priam, was able to close the performance gap between them. Priam closed its doors in 1990. The second example occurred in the next disruptive generation. Seagate Technology was the second in the industry to develop a 3.5-inch drive in 1984. Analysts at one point had speculated that Seagate might ship 3.5-inch drives as early as 1985; and indeed, Seagate showed a 10 MB model at the fall 1985 Comdex Show. When Seagate still had not shipped a 3.5-inch drive by late 1986, CEO Al Shugart explained, "So far, there just isn't a big enough market for it, as yet."13 In 1987, when the 3.5- inch market at $1.6 billion had gotten "big enough to be interesting," Seagate finally launched its 111 offering. By 1991, however, even though Seagate had by then built substantial volume in 3.5-inch drives, it had not yet succeeded in selling a single drive to a maker of portable computers: Its models were all sold into the desktop market, defensively cannibalizing its sales of 5.25-inch drives. Why? One likely reason for this phenomenon is that Conner Peripherals, which pioneered and maintained the lead in selling 3.5-inch drives to portable computer makers, fundamentally changed the way drive makers had to approach the portables market. As one Conner executive described it, From the beginning of the OEM disk drive industry, product development had proceeded in three sequential steps. First you designed the drive; then you made it; and then you sold it. We changed all that. We first sell the drives; then we design them; and then we build them.14 In other words, Conner set a pattern whereby drives for the portable computer market were customdesigned for major customers. And it refined a set of capabilities in its marketing, engineering, and manufacturing processes that were tailored to that pattern.15 Said another Conner executive, "Seagate was never able to figure out how to sell drives in the portable market. They just never got it."16 CASE STUDY: GIVING SMALL OPPORTUNITIES TO SMALL ORGANIZATIONS Every innovation is difficult. That difficulty is compounded immeasurably, however, when a project is embedded in an organization in which most people are continually questioning why the project is being done at all. Projects make sense to people if they address the needs of important customers, if they positively impact the organization's needs for profit and growth, and if participating in the project enhances the career opportunities of talented employees. When a project doesn't have these characteristics, its manager spends much time and energy justifying why it merits resources and cannot manage the project as effectively. Frequently in such circumstances, the best people do not want to be associated with the project—and when things get tight, projects viewed as nonessential are the first to be canceled or postponed. Executives can give an enormous boost to a project's probability of success, therefore, when they ensure that it is being executed in an environment in which everyone involved views the endeavor as crucial to the organization's future growth and profitability. Under these conditions, when the inevitable disappointments, unforeseen problems, and schedule slippages occur, the organization will be more likely to find ways to muster whatever is required to solve the problem. As we have seen, a project to commercialize a disruptive technology in a small, emerging market is very unlikely to be considered essential to success in a large company; small markets don't solve the growth problems of big companies. Rather than continually working to convince and remind everyone that the small, disruptive technology might someday be significant or that it is at least strategically important, large companies should seek to embed the project in an organization that is small enough to be motivated by the opportunity offered by a disruptive technology in its early years. This can be done either by spinning out an independent organization or by acquiring an appropriately small company. Expecting achievement-driven employees in a large organization to devote a critical mass of resources, attention, and energy to a disruptive project targeted at a small and poorly defined market is equivalent to flapping one's arms in an effort to fly: It denies an important tendency in the way organizations work.17 112 There are many success stories to the credit of this approach. Control Data, for example, which had essentially missed the 8-inch disk drive generation, sent a group to Oklahoma City to commercialize its 5.25-inch drive. In addition to CDC's need to escape the power of its mainstream customers, the firm explicitly wanted to create an organization whose size matched the opportunity. "We needed an organization," reflected one manager, "that could get excited about a $50,000 order. In Minneapolis [which derived nearly $1 billion from the sale of 14-inch drives in the mainframe market] you needed a million-dollar order just to turn anyone's head." CDC's Oklahoma City venture proved to be a significant success. Another way of matching the size of an organization to the size of the opportunity is to acquire a small company within which to incubate the disruptive technology. This is how Allen Bradley negotiated its very successful disruptive transition from mechanical to electronic motor controls. For decades the Allen Bradley Company (AB) in Milwaukee has been the undisputed leader in the motor controls industry, making heavy-duty, sophisticated switches that turn large electric motors off and on and protect them from overloads and surges in current. AB's customers were makers of machine tools and cranes as well as contractors who installed fans and pumps for industrial and commercial heating, ventilating, and air conditioning (HVAC) systems. Motor controls were electromechanical devices that operated on the same principle as residential light switches, although on a larger scale. In sophisticated machine tools and HVAC systems, electric motors and their controls were often linked, through systems of electromechanical relay switches, to turn on and off in particular sequences and under particular conditions. Because of the value of the equipment they controlled and the high cost of equipment downtime, controls were required to be rugged, capable of turning on and off millions of times and of withstanding the vibrations and dirt that characterized the environments in which they were used. In 1968, a startup company, Modicon, began selling electronic programmable motor controls—a disruptive technology from the point of view of mainstream users of electromechanical controls. Texas Instruments (TI) entered the fray shortly thereafter with its own electronic controller. Because early electronic controllers lacked the real and perceived ruggedness and robustness for harsh environments of the hefty AB-type controllers, Modicon and TI were unable to sell their products to mainstream machine tool makers and HVAC contractors. As performance was measured in the mainstream markets, electronic products underperformed conventional controllers, and few mainstream customers needed the programmable flexibility offered by electronic controllers. As a consequence, Modicon and TI were forced to cultivate an emerging market for programmable controllers: the market for factory automation. Customers in this emerging market were not equipment manufacturers, but equipment users, such as Ford and General Motors, who were just beginning their attempt to integrate pieces of automatic manufacturing equipment. Of the five leading manufacturers of electromechanical motor controls—Allen Bradley, Square D, Cutler Hammer, General Electric, and Westinghouse—only Allen Bradley retained a strong market position as programmable electronic controls improved in ruggedness and began to invade the core motor control markets. Allen Bradley entered the electronic controller market just two years after Modicon and built a market-leading position in the new technology within a few years, even as it kept its strength in its old electromechanical products. It subsequently transformed itself into a major supplier of electronic controllers for factory automation. The other four companies, by contrast, introduced electronic controllers much later and subsequently either exited the controller business or were reduced to weak positions. From a capabilities perspective this is a surprising outcome, because 113 General Electric and Westinghouse had much deeper expertise in microelectronics technologies at that time than did Allen Bradley, which had no institutional experience in the technology. What did Allen Bradley do differently? In 1969, just one year after Modicon entered the market, AB executives bought a 25 percent interest in Information Instruments, Inc., a fledgling programmable controller start-up based in Ann Arbor, Michigan. The following year it purchased outright a nascent division of Bunker Ramo, which was focused on programmable electronic controls and their emerging markets. AB combined these acquisitions into a single unit and maintained it as a business separate from its mainstream electromechanical products operation in Milwaukee. Over time, the electronics products have significantly eaten into the electromechanical controller business, as one AB division attacked the other.18 By contrast, each of the other four companies tried to manage its electronic controller businesses from within its mainstream electromechanical divisions, whose customers did not initially need or want electronic controls. Each failed to develop a viable position in the new technology. Johnson & Johnson has with great success followed a strategy similar to Allen Bradley's in dealing with disruptive technologies such as endoscopic surgical equipment and disposable contact lenses. Though its total revenues amount to more than $20 billion, J&J comprises 160 autonomously operating companies, which range from its huge MacNeil and Janssen pharmaceuticals companies to small companies with annual revenues of less than $20 million. Johnson & Johnson's strategy is to launch products of disruptive technologies through very small companies acquired for that purpose.

It is not crucial for managers pursuing growth and competitive advantage to be leaders in every element of their business. In sustaining technologies, in fact, evidence strongly suggests that companies which focus on extending the performance of conventional technologies, and choose to be followers in adopting new ones, can remain strong and competitive. This is not the case with disruptive technologies, however. There are enormous returns and significant first-mover advantages associated with early entry into the emerging markets in which disruptive technologies are initially used. Disk drive manufacturers that led in commercializing disruptive technology grew at vastly greater rates than did companies that were disruptive technology followers. Despite the evidence that leadership in commercializing disruptive technologies is crucial, large, successful innovators encounter a significant dilemma in the pursuit of such leadership. In addition to dealing with the power of present customers as discussed in the last chapter, large, growth-oriented companies face the problem that small markets don't solve the near-term growth needs of large companies. The markets whose emergence is enabled by disruptive technologies all began as small ones. The first orders that the pioneering companies received in those markets were small ones. And the companies that cultivated those markets had to develop cost structures enabling them to become profitable at small scale. Each of these factors argues for a policy of implanting projects to commercialize disruptive innovations in small organizations that will view the projects as being on their critical path to growth and success, rather than as being distractions from the main business of the company.

6

Discovering New and Emerging Markets

Markets that do not exist cannot be analyzed: Suppliers and customers must discover them together. Not only are the market applications for disruptive technologies unknown at the time of their development, they are unknowable. The strategies and plans that managers formulate for confronting disruptive technological change, therefore, should be plans for learning and discovery rather than plans for execution. This is an important point to understand, because managers who believe they know a market's future will plan and invest very differently from those who recognize the uncertainties of a developing market. Most managers learn about innovation in a sustaining technology context because most technologies developed by established companies are sustaining in character. Such innovations are, by definition, targeted at known markets in which customer needs are understood. In this environment, a planned, researched approach to evaluating, developing, and marketing innovative products is not only possible, it is critical to success. What this means, however, is that much of what the best executives in successful companies have learned about managing innovation is not relevant to disruptive technologies. Most marketers, for example, have been schooled extensively, at universities and on the job, in the important art of listening to their customers, but few have any theoretical or practical training in how to discover markets that do not yet exist. The problem with this lopsided experience base is that when the same analytical and decision-making processes learned in the school of sustaining innovation are applied to enabling or disruptive technologies, the effect on the company can be paralyzing. These processes demand crisply quantified information when none exists, accurate estimates of financial returns when neither revenues nor costs can be known, and management according to detailed plans and budgets that cannot be formulated. Applying inappropriate marketing, investment, and management processes can render good companies incapable of creating the new markets in which enabling or disruptive technologies are first used.

In this chapter we shall see how experts in the disk drive industry were able to forecast the markets for sustaining technologies with stunning accuracy but had great difficulty in spotting the advent and predicting the size of new markets for disruptive innovations. Additional case histories in the motorcycle and microprocessor industries further demonstrate the uncertainty about emerging market applications for disruptive or enabling technologies, even those that, in retrospect, appear obvious. FORECASTING MARKETS FOR SUSTAINING VERSUS DISRUPTIVE TECHNOLOGIES An unusual amount of market information has been available about the disk drive industry from its earliest days—a major reason why studying it has yielded such rich insights. The primary source of 118 data, Disk/Trend Report, published annually by Disk/Trend, Inc., of Mountain View, California, lists every model of disk drive that has ever been offered for sale by any company in the world, for each of the years from 1975 to the present. It shows the month and year in which each model was first shipped, lists the performance specifications of the drive, and details the component technologies used. In addition, every manufacturer in the world shares with Disk/Trend its sales by product type, with information about what types of customers bought which drive. Editors at Disk/Trend then aggregate this data to derive the size of each narrowly defined market segment and publish a listing of the major competitors' shares, carefully guarding all proprietary data. Manufacturers in the industry find the reports so valuable that they all continue to share their proprietary data with Disk/Trend.

To facilitate comparison, the heights of the bars measuring forecast shipments were normalized to a value of 100, and the volumes actually shipped were scaled as a percentage of the forecast. Of the five 119 new architectures for which Disk/Trend's forecasts were available, the 14-inch Winchester and the 2.5- inch generation were sustaining innovations, which were sold into the same value networks as the preceding generation of drives. The other three, 5.25-, 3.5-, and 1.8-inch drives, were disruptive innovations that facilitated the emergence of new value networks. (Disk/ Trend did not publish separate forecasts for 8-inch drives.) Notice that Disk/

Trend's forecasts for the sustaining 2.5-inch and 14-inch Winchester technologies were within 8 percent and 7 percent, respectively, of what the industry actually shipped. But its estimates were off by 265 percent for 5.25-inch drives, 35 percent for 3.5-inch drives (really quite close), and 550 percent for 1.8-inch drives. Notably, the 1.8-inch drive, the forecast of which Disk/Trend missed so badly, was the first generation of drives with a primarily non-computer market. The Disk/Trend staff used the same methods to generate the forecasts for sustaining architectures as they did for disruptive ones: interviewing leading customers and industry experts, trend analysis, economic modeling, and so on. The techniques that worked so extraordinarily well when applied to sustaining technologies, however, clearly failed badly when applied to markets or applications that did not yet exist. IDENTIFYING THE MARKET FOR THE HP 1.3-INCH KITTYHAWK DRIVE Differences in the forecastablity of sustaining versus disruptive technologies profoundly affected Hewlett-Packard's efforts to forge a market for its revolutionary, disruptive 1.3-inch Kittyhawk disk drive.1 In 1991, Hewlett-Packard's Disk Memory Division (DMD), based in Boise, Idaho, generated about $600 million in disk drive revenues for its $20 billion parent company. That year a group of DMD employees conceived of a tiny, 1.3-inch 20 MB drive, which they code-named Kittyhawk. This was indeed a radical program for HP: The smallest drive previously made by DMD had been 3.5- inches, and DMD had been one of the last in the industry to introduce one. The 1.3-inch Kittyhawk represented a significant leapfrog for the company—and, most notably, was HP's first attempt to lead in a disruptive technology. For the project to make sense in a large organization with ambitious growth plans, HP executives mandated that Kittyhawk's revenues had to ramp to $150 million within three years. Fortunately for Kittyhawk's proponents, however, a significant market for this tiny drive loomed on the horizon: handheld palm-top computers, or personal digital assistants (PDAs). Kittyhawk's sponsors, after studying projections for this market, decided that they could scale the revenue ramp that had been set for them. They consulted a market research firm, which confirmed HP's belief that the market for Kittyhawk would indeed be substantial. HP's marketers developed deep relationships with senior executives at major companies in the computer industry, for example, Motorola, ATT, IBM, Apple, Microsoft, Intel, NCR, and HewlettPackard itself, as well as at a host of lesser-known startup companies. All had placed substantial product development bets on the PDA market. Many of their products were designed with Kittyhawk's features in mind, and Kittyhawk's design in turn reflected these customers' well-researched needs. The Kittyhawk team concluded that developing a drive that met these customers' requirements would be a demanding but feasible technological stretch, and they launched an aggressive twelve-month effort to develop the tiny device. The result, shown in Figure 7.2, was impressive. The first version packed 20 120 MB, and a second model, introduced a year later, stored 40 MB. To meet the ruggedness demanded in its target market of PDAs and electronic notebooks, Kittyhawk was equipped with an impact sensor similar to those used in automobile airbag crash sensors and could withstand a three-foot drop onto concrete without data loss. It was designed to sell initially at $250 per unit. Although Kittyhawk's technical development went according to plan, the development of applications for it did not. The PDA market failed to materialize substantially, as sales of Apple's Newton and competing devices fell far short of aspirations. This surprised many of the computer industry experts whose opinions HP's marketers had worked so hard to synthesize. During its first two years on the market, Kittyhawk logged just a fraction of the sales that had been forecast. The sales achieved might have initially satisfied startup companies and venture capitalists, but for HP's management, the volumes were far below expectations and far too small to satisfy DMD's need to grow and gain overall market share. Even more surprising, the applications that contributed most significantly to Kittyhawk's sales were not in computers at all. They were Japanese-language portable word processors, miniature cash registers, electronic cameras, and industrial scanners, none of which had figured in Kittyhawk's original marketing plans.

Even more frustrating, as the second anniversary of Kittyhawk's launch approached, were the inquiries received by HP marketers from companies making mass-market video game systems to buy very large volumes of Kittyhawk—if HP could make a version available at a lower price point. These companies had been aware of Kittyhawk for two years, but they reported that it had taken some time for them to see what could be done with a storage device so small. To a significant extent, HP had designed Kittyhawk to be a sustaining technology for mobile computing. Along many of the metrics of value in that application—small size, low weight and power consumption, and ruggedness—Kittyhawk constituted a discontinuous sustaining improvement relative 121 to 2.5- and 1.8-inch drives. Only in capacity (which HP had pushed as far as possible) was Kittyhawk deficient.

The large inquiries and orders that finally began arriving for the Kittyhawk, however, were for a truly disruptive product: something priced at $50 per unit and with limited functionality. For these applications, a capacity of 10 MB would have been perfectly adequate. Unfortunately, because HP had positioned the drive with the expensive features needed for the PDA market rather than designing it as a truly disruptive product, it simply could not meet the price required by home video game manufacturers. Having invested so aggressively to hit its original targets as defined by the PDA application, management had little patience and no money to redesign a simpler, defeatured 1.3-inch drive that fit the market applications that had finally become clear. HP withdrew Kittyhawk from the market in late 1994. The HP project managers concede in retrospect that their most serious mistake in managing the Kittyhawk initiative was to act as if their forecasts about the market were right, rather than as if they were wrong. They had invested aggressively in manufacturing capacity for producing the volumes forecast for the PDA market and had incorporated design features, such as the shock sensor, that were crucial to acceptance in the PDA market they had so carefully researched. Such planning and investment is crucial to success in a sustaining technology, but, the managers reflected, it was not right for a disruptive product like Kittyhawk. If they had the opportunity to launch Kittyhawk all over again, they would assume that neither they nor anyone else knew for sure what kinds of customers would want it or in what volumes. This would lead them toward a much more exploratory, flexible approach toward product design and investment in manufacturing capacity; they would, given another chance, feel their way into the market, leaving enough resources to redirect their program if necessary and building upon what they learned on the way. Hewlett-Packard's disk drive makers are not the only ones, of course, who behaved as if they knew what the market for a disruptive technology would be. They are in stellar company, as the following case histories show. HONDA'S INVASION OF THE NORTH AMERICAN MOTORCYCLE INDUSTRY Honda's success in attacking and dominating the North American and European motorcycle markets has been cited as a superb example of clear strategic thinking coupled with aggressive and coherent execution. According to these accounts, Honda employed a deliberate manufacturing strategy based on an experience curve in which it cut prices, built volume, aggressively reduced costs, cut prices some more, reduced costs further, and built an unassailable volume-based low-cost manufacturing position in the motorcycle market.

Honda then used that base to move upmarket and ultimately blew all established motorcycle manufacturers out of the market except for Harley-Davidson and BMW, which barely survived.2 Honda combined this manufacturing triumph with a clever product design, catchy advertising, and a convenient, broad-based distributor/retailer network tailored to the informal cyclists who constituted Honda's core customer base. Told in this manner, Honda's history is a tale of strategic brilliance and operational excellence that all managers dream will be told about them someday. The reality of Honda's achievement, as recounted by the Honda employees who were managing the business at the time, however, is quite different.3 During Japan's years of post-war reconstruction and poverty, Honda had emerged as a supplier of small, rugged motorized bicycles that were used by distributors and retailers in congested urban areas 122 to make small deliveries to local customers. Honda developed considerable expertise in designing small, efficient engines for these bikes. Its Japanese market sales grew from an initial annual volume of 1,200 units in 1949 to 285,000 units in 1959. Honda's executives were eager to exploit the company's low labor costs to export motorbikes to North America, but there was no equivalent market there for its popular Japanese "Supercub" delivery bike. Honda's research showed that Americans used motorcyles primarily for over-the-road distance driving in which size, power, and speed were the most highly valued product attributes. Accordingly, Honda engineers designed a fast, powerful motorcycle specifically for the American market, and in 1959 Honda dispatched three employees to Los Angeles to begin marketing efforts. To save living expenses, the three shared an apartment, and each brought with him a Supercub bike to provide cheap transportation around the city. The venture was a frustrating experience from the beginning. Honda's products offered no advantage to prospective customers other than cost, and most motorcycle dealers refused to accept the unproven product line. When the team finally succeeded in finding some dealers and selling a few hundred units, the results were disastrous. Honda's understanding of engine design turned out not to be transferable to highway applications, in which bikes were driven at high speeds for extended periods: The engines sprung oil leaks and the clutches wore out. Honda's expenses in air-freighting the warrantied replacement motorcycles between Japan and Los Angeles nearly sunk the company. Meanwhile, one Saturday, Kihachiro Kawashima, the Honda executive in charge of the North American venture, decided to vent his frustrations by taking his Supercub into the hills east of Los Angeles.

It helped: He felt better after zipping around in the dirt. A few weeks later he sought relief dirt-biking again. Eventually he invited his two colleagues to join him on their Supercubs. Their neighbors and others who saw them zipping around the hills began inquiring where they could buy those cute little bikes, and the trio obliged by special-ordering Supercub models for them from Japan. This private use of what became known as off-road dirt bikes continued for a couple of years. At one point a Sears buyer tried to order Supercubs for the company's outdoor power equipment departments, but Honda ignored the opportunity, preferring to focus on selling large, powerful, over-the-road cycles, a strategy that continued to be unsuccessful. Finally, as more and more people clamored for their own little Honda Supercubs to join their dirtbiking friends, the potential for a very different market dawned on Honda's U.S. team: Maybe there was an undeveloped off-the-road recreational motorbike market in North America for which—quite by accident—the company's little 50cc Supercub was nicely suited. Although it took much arguing and arm-twisting, the Los Angeles team ultimately convinced corporate management in Japan that while the company's large bike strategy was doomed to failure, another quite different opportunity to create a totally new market segment merited pursuit. Once the small-bike strategy was formally adopted, the team found that securing dealers for the Supercub was an even more vexing challenge than it had been for its big bikes. There just weren't any retailers selling that class of product. Ultimately, Honda persuaded a few sporting goods dealers to take on its line of motorbikes, and as they began to promote the bikes successfully, Honda's innovative distribution strategy was born. Honda had no money for a sophisticated advertising campaign. But a UCLA student who had gone dirt-biking with his friends came up with the advertising slogan, "You meet the nicest people on a Honda," for a paper he wrote in an advertising course. Encouraged by his teacher, he sold the idea to an advertising agency, which then convinced Honda to use it in what became an award-winning 123 advertising campaign. These serendipitous events were, of course, followed by truly world-class design engineering and manufacturing execution, which enabled Honda to repeatedly lower its prices as it improved its product quality and increased its production volumes. Honda's 50cc motorbike was a disruptive technology in the North American market. The rank-ordering of product attributes that Honda's customers employed in their product decision making defined for Honda a very different value network than the established network in which Harley-

Davidson, BMW, and other traditional motorcycle makers had competed. From its low-cost manufacturing base for reliable motorbikes, using a strategy reminiscent of the upmarket invasions described earlier in disk drives, steel, excavators, and retailing, Honda turned its sights upmarket, introducing between 1970 and 1988 a series of bikes with progressively more powerful engines. For a time in the late 1960s and early 1970s, Harley attempted to compete head-on with Honda and to capitalize on the expanding low-end market by producing a line of small-engine (150 to 300 cc) bikes acquired from the Italian motorcycle maker Aeromecchania. Harley attempted to sell the bikes through its North American dealer network. Although Honda's manufacturing prowess clearly disadvantaged Harley in this effort, a primary cause of Harley's failure to establish a strong presence in the small-bike value network was the opposition of its dealer network. Their profit margins were far greater on highend bikes, and many of them felt the small machines compromised Harley-Davidson's image with their core customers. Recall from chapter 2 the finding that within a given value network, the disk drive companies and their computer-manufacturing customers had developed very similar economic models or cost structures, which determined the sorts of business that appeared profitable to them. We see the same phenomenon here. Within their value network, the economics of Harley's dealers drove them to favor the same type of business that Harley had come to favor. Their coexistence within the value network made it difficult for either Harley or its dealers to exit the network through its bottom. In the late 1970s Harley gave in and repositioned itself at the very high end of the motorcycle market—a strategy reminiscent of Seagate's repositioning in disk drives, and of the upmarket retreats of the cable excavator companies and the integrated steel mills. Interestingly, Honda proved just as inaccurate in estimating how large the potential North American motorcycle market was as it had been in understanding what it was. Its initial aspirations upon entry in 1959 had been to capture 10 percent of a market estimated at 550,000 units per year with annual growth of 5 percent. By 1975 the market had grown 16 percent per year to 5,000,000 annual units— units that came largely from an application that Honda could not have foreseen.4 INTEL'S DISCOVERY OF THE MICROPROCESSOR MARKET Intel Corporation, whose founders launched the company in 1969 based on their pioneering development of metal-on-silicon (MOS) technology to produce the world's first dynamic random access memory (DRAM) integrated circuits, had become by 1995 one of the world's most profitable major companies. Its storied success is even more remarkable because, when its initial leadership position in the DRAM market began crumbling between 1978 and 1986 under the onslaught of 124 Japanese semiconductor manufacturers, Intel transformed itself from a second-tier DRAM company into the world's dominant microprocessor manufacturer. How did Intel do it? Intel developed the original microprocessor under a contract development arrangement with a Japanese calculator manufacturer. When the project was over, Intel's engineering team persuaded company executives to purchase the microprocessor patent from the calculator maker, which owned it under the terms of its contract with Intel. Intel had no explicit strategy for building a market for this new microprocessor; the company simply sold the chip to whoever seemed to be able to use it. Mainstream as they seem today, microprocessors were disruptive technologies when they first emerged. They were capable only of limited functionality, compared to the complex logic circuits that constituted the central processing units of large computers in the 1960s. But they were small and simple, and they enabled affordable logic and computation in applications where this previously had not been feasible. Through the 1970s, as competition in the DRAM market intensified, margins began to decline on Intel's DRAM revenues while margins on its microprocessor product line, where there was less competition, stayed robust. Intel's system for allocating production capacity operated according to a formula whereby capacity was committed in proportion to the gross margins earned by each product line. The system therefore imperceptibly began diverting investment capital and manufacturing capacity away from the DRAM business and into microprocessors—without an explicit management decision to do so.5 In fact, Intel senior management continued to focus most of its own attention and energy on DRAM, even while the company's resource allocation processes were gradually implementing an exit from that business. This de facto strategy shift, driven by Intel's autonomously operating resource allocation process, was fortuitous. Because so little was known of the microprocessor market at that time, explicit analysis would have provided little justification for a bold move into microprocessors. Gordon Moore, Intel cofounder and chairman, for example, recalled that IBM's choice of the Intel 8088 microprocessor as the "brain" of its new personal computer was viewed within Intel as a "small design win."6 Even after IBM's stunning success with its personal computers, Intel's internal forecast of the potential applications for the company's next-generation 286 chip did not include personal computers in its list of the fifty highest-volume applications.7 In retrospect, the application of microprocessors to personal computers is an obvious match. But in the heat of the battle, of the many applications in which microprocessors might have been used, even a management team as astute as Intel's could not know which would emerge as the most important and what volumes and profits it would yield. UNPREDICTABILITY AND DOWNWARD IMMOBILITY IN ESTABLISHED FIRMS The reaction of some managers to the difficulty of correctly planning the markets for disruptive technologies is to work harder and plan smarter. While this approach works for sustaining innovations, it denies the evidence about the nature of disruptive ones. Amid all the uncertainty surrounding disruptive technologies, managers can always count on one anchor: Experts' forecasts will always be wrong. It is simply impossible to predict with any useful degree of precision how disruptive products will be used or how large their markets will be. An important corollary is that, because markets for 125 disruptive technologies are unpredictable, companies' initial strategies for entering these markets will generally be wrong. How does this statement square with the findings presented in Table 6.1, which showed a stunning difference in the posterior probabilities of success between firms that entered new, emerging value networks (37 percent) and those that entered existing value networks (6 percent)? If markets cannot be predicted in advance, how can firms that target them be more successful? Indeed, when I have shown the matrix in Table 6.1 to managerial audiences, they are quite astonished by the differences in the magnitudes and probabilities of success. But it is clear that the managers don't believe that the results can be generalized to their own situations. The findings violate their intuitive sense that creating new markets is a genuinely risky business.8 Failed Ideas versus Failed Businesses The case studies reviewed in this chapter suggest a resolution to this puzzle. There is a big difference between the failure of an idea and the failure of a firm. Many of the ideas prevailing at Intel about where the disruptive microprocessor could be used were wrong; fortunately, Intel had not expended all of its resources implementing wrong-headed marketing plans while the right market direction was still unknowable. As a company, Intel survived many false starts in its search for the major market for microprocessors. Similarly, Honda's idea about how to enter the North American motorcycle market was wrong, but the company didn't deplete its resources pursuing its big-bike strategy and was able to invest aggressively in the winning strategy after it had emerged. Hewlett-Packard's Kittyhawk team was not as fortunate. Believing they had identified the winning strategy, its managers spent their budget on a product design and the manufacturing capacity for a market application that never emerged. When the ultimate applications for the tiny drive ultimately began to coalesce, the Kittyhawk team had no resources left to pursue them. Research has shown, in fact, that the vast majority of successful new business ventures abandoned their original business strategies when they began implementing their initial plans and learned what would and would not work in the market.9 The dominant difference between successful ventures and failed ones, generally, is not the astuteness of their original strategy. Guessing the right strategy at the outset isn't nearly as important to success as conserving enough resources (or having the relationships with trusting backers or investors) so that new business initiatives get a second or third stab at getting it right. Those that run out of resources or credibility before they can iterate toward a viable strategy are the ones that fail. Failed Ideas and Failed Managers In most companies, however, individual managers don't have the luxury of surviving a string of trials and errors in pursuit of the strategy that works. Rightly or wrongly, individual managers in most organizations believe that they cannot fail: If they champion a project that fails because the initial marketing plan was wrong, it will constitute a blotch on their track record, blocking their rise through the organization. Because failure is intrinsic to the process of finding new markets for disruptive technologies, the inability or unwillingness of individual managers to put their careers at risk acts as a 126 powerful deterrent to the movement of established firms into the value networks created by those technologies. As Joseph Bower observed in his classic study of the resource allocation process at a major chemical company, "Pressure from the market reduces both the probability and the cost of being wrong." 10 Bower's observation is consistent with the findings in this book about the disk drive industry. When demand for an innovation was assured, as was the case with sustaining technologies, the industry's established leaders were capable of placing huge, long, and risky bets to develop whatever technology was required. When demand was not assured, as was the case in disruptive technologies, the established firms could not even make the technologically straightforward bets required to commercialize such innovations. That is why 65 percent of the companies entering the disk drive industry attempted to do so in an established, rather than emerging market. Discovering markets for emerging technologies inherently involves failure, and most individual decision makers find it very difficult to risk backing a project that might fail because the market is not there.

Plans to Learn versus Plans to Execute Because failure is intrinsic to the search for initial market applications for disruptive technologies, managers need an approach very different from what they would take toward a sustaining technology. In general, for sustaining technologies, plans must be made before action is taken, forecasts can be accurate, and customer inputs can be reasonably reliable. Careful planning, followed by aggressive execution, is the right formula for success in sustaining technology. But in disruptive situations, action must be taken before careful plans are made. Because much less can be known about what markets need or how large they can become, plans must serve a very different purpose: They must be plans for learning rather than plans for implementation. By approaching a disruptive business with the mindset that they can't know where the market is, managers would identify what critical information about new markets is most necessary and in what sequence that information is needed. Project and business plans would mirror those priorities, so that key pieces of information would be created, or important uncertainties resolved, before expensive commitments of capital, time, and money were required.

7

How to Appraise Your Organization's Capabilities and Disabilities

When managers assign employees to tackle a critical innovation, they instinctively work to match the requirements of the job with the capabilities of the individuals whom they charge to do it. In evaluating whether an employee is capable of successfully executing a job, managers will assess whether he or she has the requisite knowledge, judgment, skill, perspective, and energy. Managers will also assess the employee's values—the criteria by which he or she tends to decide what should and shouldn't be done. Indeed, the hallmark of a great manager is the ability to identify the right person for the right job, and to train his or her employees so that they have the capabilities to succeed at the jobs they are given. Unfortunately, some managers don't think as rigorously about whether their organizations have the capability to successfully execute jobs that may be given to them. Frequently, they assume that if the people working on a project individually have the requisite capabilities to get the job done well, then the organization in which they work will also have the same capability to succeed. This often is not the case. One could take two sets of identically capable people and put them to work in two different organizations, and what they accomplish would likely be significantly different. This is because organizations themselves, independent of the people and other resources in them, have capabilities. To succeed consistently, good managers need to be skilled not just in choosing, training, and motivating the right people for the right job, but in choosing, building, and preparing the right organization for the job as well. The purpose of this chapter is to describe the theory that lies behind the empirical observations made in chapters 5, 6, and 7—in particular, the observation that the only companies that succeeded in addressing disruptive technology were those that created independent organizations whose size matched the size of the opportunity. The notion that organizations have "core competencies" has been a popular one for much of the last decade.1 In practice, however, most managers have found that the concept is sufficiently vague that some supposed "competence" can be cited in support of a bewildering variety of innovation proposals. This chapter brings greater precision to the core competence concept, by presenting a framework to help managers understand, when they are confronted with a necessary change, whether the organizations over which they preside are competent or incompetent of tackling the challenges that lie ahead. AN ORGANIZATIONAL CAPABILITIES FRAMEWORK Three classes of factors affect what an organization can and cannot do: its resources, its processes, and its values. When asking what sorts of innovations their organizations are and are not likely to be able to implement successfully, managers can learn a lot about capabilities by disaggregating their answers into these three categories.2 130 Resources Resources are the most visible of the factors that contribute to what an organization can and cannot do. Resources include people, equipment, technology, product designs, brands, information, cash, and relationships with suppliers, distributors, and customers. Resources are usually things, or assets—they can be hired and fired, bought and sold, depreciated or enhanced. They often can be transferred across the boundaries of organizations much more readily than can processes and values. Without doubt, access to abundant and high-quality resources enhances an organization's chances of coping with change. Resources are the things that managers most instinctively identify when assessing whether their organizations can successfully implement changes that confront them. Yet resource analysis clearly does not tell a sufficient story about capabilities. Indeed, we could deal identical sets of resources to two different organizations, and what they created from those resources would likely be very different—because the capabilities to transform inputs into goods and services of greater value reside in the organization's processes and values. Processes Organizations create value as employees transform inputs of resources—people, equipment, technology, product designs, brands, information, energy, and cash—into products and services of greater worth. The patterns of interaction, coordination, communication, and decision-making through which they accomplish these transformations are processes. 3 Processes include not just manufacturing processes, but those by which product development, procurement, market research, budgeting, planning, employee development and compensation, and resource allocation are accomplished. Processes differ not only in their purpose, but also in their visibility. Some processes are "formal," in the sense that they are explicitly defined, visibly documented, and consciously followed. Other processes are "informal," in that they are habitual routines or ways of working that have evolved over time, which people follow simply because they work—or because "That's the way we do things around here." Still other methods of working and interacting have proven so effective for so long that people unconsciously follow them—they constitute the culture of the organization. Whether they are formal, informal, or cultural, however, processes define how an organization transforms the sorts of inputs listed above into things of greater value. Processes are defined or evolve de facto to address specific tasks. This means that when managers use a process to execute the tasks for which it was designed, it is likely to perform efficiently. But when the same, seemingly efficient process is employed to tackle a very different task, it is likely to seem slow, bureaucratic, and inefficient. In other words, a process that defines a capability in executing a certain task concurrently defines disabilities in executing other tasks.4 The reason good managers strive for focus in their organizations is that processes and tasks can be readily aligned.5 One of the dilemmas of management is that, by their very nature, processes are established so that employees perform recurrent tasks in a consistent way, time after time. To ensure consistency, they are 131 meant not to change—or if they must change, to change through tightly controlled procedures. This means that the very mechanisms through which organizations create value are intrinsically inimical to change. Some of the most crucial processes to examine as capabilities or disabilities aren't the obvious valueadding processes involved in logistics, development, manufacturing, and customer service. Rather, they are the enabling or background processes that support investment decision-making. As we saw in chapter 7, the processes that render good companies incapable of responding to change are often those that define how market research is habitually done; how such analysis is translated into financial projections; how plans and budgets are negotiated and how those numbers are delivered; and so on. These typically inflexible processes are where many organizations' most serious disabilities in coping with change reside. Values The third class of factors that affect what an organization can or cannot accomplish is its values. The values of an organization are the criteria by which decisions about priorities are made. Some corporate values are ethical in tone, such as those that guide decisions to ensure patient well-being at Johnson & Johnson or that guide decisions about plant safety at Alcoa. But within the Resources-Processes-Values (RPV) framework, values have a broader meaning. An organization's values are the standards by which employees make prioritization decisions—by which they judge whether an order is attractive or unattractive; whether a customer is more important or less important; whether an idea for a new product is attractive or marginal; and so on. Prioritization decisions are made by employees at every level. At the executive tiers, they often take the form of decisions to invest or not invest in new products, services, and processes. Among salespeople, they consist of on-the-spot, day-to-day decisions about which products to push with customers and which not to emphasize. The larger and more complex a company becomes, the more important it is for senior managers to train employees at every level to make independent decisions about priorities that are consistent with the strategic direction and the business model of the company. A key metric of good management, in fact, is whether such clear and consistent values have permeated the organization.6 Clear, consistent, and broadly understood values, however, also define what an organization cannot do. A company's values, by necessity, must reflect its cost structure or its business model, because these define the rules its employees must follow in order for the company to make money. If, for example, the structure of a company's overhead costs requires it to achieve gross profit margins of 40 percent, a powerful value or decision rule will have evolved that encourages middle managers to kill ideas that promise gross margins below 40 percent. This means that such an organization would be incapable of successfully commercializing projects targeting low-margin markets. At the same time, another organization's values, driven by a very different cost structure, might enable or facilitate the success of the very same project. The values of successful firms tend to evolve in a predictable fashion in at least two dimensions. The first relates to acceptable gross margins. As companies add features and functionality to their products and services in order to capture more attractive customers in premium tiers of their markets, they often add overhead cost. As a result, gross margins that at one point were quite attractive, at a later point seem unattractive. Their values change. For example, Toyota entered the North American market with 132 its Corona model—a product targeting the lowest-priced tiers of the market. As the entry tier of the market became crowded with look-alike models from Nissan, Honda, and Mazda, competition among equally low-cost competitors drove down profit margins. Toyota developed more sophisticated cars targeted at higher tiers of the market in order to improve its margins. Its Corolla, Camry, Previa, Avalon, and Lexus families of cars have been introduced in response to the same competitive pressures—it kept its margins healthy by migrating up-market. In the process, Toyota has had to add costs to its operation to design, build, and support cars of this caliber. It progressively deemphasized the entry-level tiers of the market, having found the margins it could earn there to be unattractive, given its changed cost structure. Nucor Steel, the leading minimill that led the up-market charge against the integrated mills that was recounted in chapter 4, likewise has experienced a change in values. As it has managed the center of gravity in its product line up-market from re-bar to angle iron to structural beams and finally to sheet steel, it has begun to decidedly deemphasize re-bar—the product that had been its bread and butter in its earlier years. The second dimension along which values predictably change relates to how big a business has to be in order to be interesting. Because a company's stock price represents the discounted present value of its projected earnings stream, most managers typically feel compelled not just to maintain growth, but to maintain a constant rate of growth. In order for a $40 million company to grow 25 percent, it needs to find $10 million in new business the next year. For a $40 billion company to grow 25 percent, it needs to find $10 billion in new business the next year. The size of market opportunity that will solve each of these companies' needs for growth is very different. As noted in chapter 6, an opportunity that excites a small organization isn't big enough to be interesting to a very large one. One of the bittersweet rewards of success is, in fact, that as companies become large, they literally lose the capability to enter small emerging markets. This disability is not because of a change in the resources within the companies— their resources typically are vast. Rather, it is because their values change. Executives and Wall Street financiers who engineer megamergers among already huge companies in order to achieve cost savings need to account for the impact of these actions on the resultant companies' values. Although their merged organizations might have more resources to throw at innovation problems, their commercial organizations tend to lose their appetites for all but the biggest blockbuster opportunities. Huge size constitutes a very real disability in managing innovation. In many ways, Hewlett-Packard's recent decision to split itself into two companies is rooted in its recognition of this problem. THE RELATIONSHIP BETWEEN PROCESSES AND VALUES, AND SUCCESS IN ADDRESSING SUSTAINING VS. DISRUPTIVE TECHNOLOGIES The resources-processes-values (RPV) framework has been a useful tool for me to understand the findings from my research relating to the differences in companies' track records in sustaining and disruptive technologies. Recall that we identified 116 new technologies that were introduced in the industry's history. Of these, 111 were sustaining technologies, in that their impact was to improve the performance of disk drives. Some of these were incremental improvements while others, such as magneto-resistive heads, represented discontinuous leaps forward in performance. In all 111 cases of sustaining technology, the companies that led in developing and introducing the new technology were 133 the companies that had led in the old technology. The success rate of the established firms in developing and adopting sustaining technologies was 100 percent. The other five of these 116 technologies were disruptive innovations—in each case, smaller disk drives that were slower and had lower capacity than those used in the mainstream market. There was no new technology involved in these disruptive products. Yet none of the industry's leading companies remained atop the industry after these disruptive innovations entered the market—their batting average was zero. Why such markedly different batting averages when playing the sustaining versus disruptive games? The answer lies in the RPV framework of organizational capabilities. The industry leaders developed and introduced sustaining technologies over and over again. Month after month, year after year, as they introduced new and improved products in order to gain an edge over the competition, the leading companies developed processes for evaluating the technological potential and assessing their customers' needs for alternative sustaining technologies. In the parlance of this chapter, the organizations developed a capability for doing these things, which resided in their processes. Sustaining technology investments also fit the values of the leading companies, in that they promised higher margins from better products sold to their leading-edge customers. On the other hand, the disruptive innovations occurred so intermittently that no company had a routinized process for handling them. Furthermore, because the disruptive products promised lower profit margins per unit sold and could not be used by their best customers, these innovations were inconsistent with the leading companies' values. The leading disk drive companies had the resources— the people, money, and technology—required to succeed at both sustaining and disruptive technologies. But their processes and values constituted disabilities in their efforts to succeed at disruptive technologies. Large companies often surrender emerging growth markets because smaller, disruptive companies are actually more capable of pursuing them. Though start-ups lack resources, it doesn't matter. Their values can embrace small markets, and their cost structures can accommodate lower margins. Their market research and resource allocation processes allow managers to proceed intuitively rather than having to be backed up by careful research and analysis, presented in PowerPoint. All of these advantages add up to enormous opportunity or looming disaster—depending upon your perspective. Managers who face the need to change or innovate, therefore, need to do more than assign the right resources to the problem. They need to be sure that the organization in which those resources will be working is itself capable of succeeding—and in making that assessment, managers must scrutinize whether the organization's processes and values fit the problem. THE MIGRATION OF CAPABILITIES In the start-up stages of an organization, much of what gets done is attributable to its resources—its people. The addition or departure of a few key people can have a profound influence on its success. Over time, however, the locus of the organization's capabilities shifts toward its processes and values. As people work together successfully to address recurrent tasks, processes become defined. And as the business model takes shape and it becomes clear which types of business need to be accorded highest priority, values coalesce. In fact, one reason that many soaring young companies flame out after they 134 go public based upon a hot initial product is that whereas their initial success was grounded in resources—the founding group of engineers—they fail to create processes that can create a sequence of hot products. An example of such flame out is the story of Avid Technology, a producer of digital editing systems for television. Avid's technology removed tedium from the video editing process. Customers loved it, and on the back of its star product, Avid stock rose from $16 at its 1993 IPO to $49 in mid-1995. However, the strains of being a one-trick pony soon surfaced as Avid was faced with a saturated market, rising inventories and receivables, and increased competition. Customers loved the product, but Avid's lack of effective processes to consistently develop new products and to control quality, delivery, and service ultimately tripped the company and sent its stock back down. In contrast, at highly successful firms such as McKinsey and Company, the processes and values have become so powerful that it almost doesn't matter which people get assigned to which project teams. Hundreds of new MBAs join the firm every year, and almost as many leave. But the company is able to crank out high-quality work year after year because its core capabilities are rooted in its processes and values rather than in its resources. I sense, however, that these capabilities of McKinsey also constitute its disabilities. The rigorously analytical, data-driven processes that help it create value for its clients in existing, relatively stable markets render it much less capable of building a strong client base among the rapidly growing companies in dynamic technology markets. In the formative stages of a company's processes and values, the actions and attitudes of the company's founder have a profound impact. The founder often has strong opinions about the way employees ought to work together to reach decisions and get things done. Founders similarly impose their views of what the organization's priorities need to be. If the founder's methods are flawed, of course, the company will likely fail. But if those methods are useful, employees will collectively experience for themselves the validity of the founder's problem-solving methodologies and criteria for decision-making. As they successfully use those methods of working together to address recurrent tasks, processes become defined. Likewise, if the company becomes financially successful by prioritizing various uses of its resources according to criteria that reflect the founder's priorities, the company's values begin to coalesce. As successful companies mature, employees gradually come to assume that the priorities they have learned to accept, and the ways of doing things and methods of making decisions that they have employed so successfully, are the right way to work. Once members of the organization begin to adopt ways of working and criteria for making decisions by assumption, rather than by conscious decision, then those processes and values come to constitute the organization's culture. 7 As companies grow from a few employees to hundreds and thousands, the challenge of getting all employees to agree on what needs to be done and how it should be done so that the right jobs are done repeatedly and consistently can be daunting for even the best managers. Culture is a powerful management tool in these situations. Culture enables employees to act autonomously and causes them to act consistently. Hence, the location of the most powerful factors that define the capabilities and disabilities of organizations migrates over time —from resources toward visible, conscious processes and values, and then toward culture. As long as the organization continues to face the same sorts of problems that its processes and values were designed to address, managing the organization is relatively straightforward. But because these factors also define what an organization cannot do, they constitute disabilities when the problems facing the company change. When the organization's capabilities reside primarily in its people, changing to address new problems is relatively simple. But when the capabilities have come to 135 reside in processes and values and especially when they have become embedded in culture, change can become extraordinarily difficult. A case in point: Did Digital Equipment have the capability to succeed in personal computers? Digital Equipment Corporation (DEC) was a spectacularly successful maker of minicomputers from the 1960s through the 1980s. One might have been tempted to assert, when the personal computer market began to coalesce in the early 1980s, that DEC's "core competence" was in building computers. But if computers were DEC's competence, why did the company stumble? Clearly, DEC had the resources to succeed in personal computers. Its engineers were routinely designing far more sophisticated computers than PCs. DEC had plenty of cash, a great brand, and strong technology. But did DEC have the processes to succeed in the personal computer business? No. The processes for designing and manufacturing minicomputers involved designing many of the key components of the computer internally and then integrating the components into proprietary configurations. The design process itself consumed two to three years for a new product model. DEC's manufacturing processes entailed making most components and assembling them in a batch mode. It sold direct to corporate engineering organizations. These processes worked extremely well in the minicomputer business. The personal computer business, in contrast, required processes through which the most cost-effective components were outsourced from the best suppliers around the globe. New computer designs, comprised of modular components, had to be completed in six- to twelve-month cycles. The computers were manufactured in high-volume assembly lines, and sold through retailers to consumers and businesses. None of these processes required to compete successfully in the personal computer business existed within DEC. In other words, although the people working at DEC, as individuals, had the abilities to design, build, and sell personal computers profitably, they were working in an organization that was incapable of doing this because its processes had been designed and had evolved to do other tasks well. The very processes that made the company capable of succeeding in one business rendered it incapable of succeeding in another. And what about DEC's values? Because of the overhead costs that were required to succeed in the minicomputer business, DEC had to adopt a set of values that essentially dictated, "If it generates 50 percent gross margins or more, it's good business. If it generates less than 40 percent margins, it's not worth doing." Management had to ensure that all employees prioritized projects according to this criterion, or the company couldn't make money. Because personal computers generated lower margins, they did not "fit" with DEC's values. The company's criteria for prioritization placed higherperformance minicomputers ahead of personal computers in the resource allocation process. And any attempts that the company made to enter the personal computer business had to target the highestmargin tiers of that market—because the financial results that might be earned in those tiers were the only ones that the company's values would tolerate. But because of the patterns noted in chapter 4—the strong tendency for competitors with low-overhead business models to migrate up-market—Digital's values rendered it incapable of pursuing a winning strategy. As we saw in chapter 5, Digital Equipment could have owned another organization whose processes and values were tailored to those required to play in the personal computer game. But the particular organization in Maynard, Massachusetts, whose extraordinary capabilities had carried the company to 136 such success in the minicomputer business, was simply incapable of succeeding in the personal computer world. CREATING CAPABILITIES TO COPE WITH CHANGE If a manager determined that an employee was incapable of succeeding at a task, he or she would either find someone else to do the job or carefully train the employee to be able to succeed. Training often works, because individuals can become skilled at multiple tasks. Despite beliefs spawned by popular change-management and reengineering programs, processes are not nearly as flexible or "trainable" as are resources—and values are even less so. The processes that make an organization good at outsourcing components cannot simultaneously make it good at developing and manufacturing components in-house. Values that focus an organization's priorities on high-margin products cannot simultaneously focus priorities on low-margin products. This is why focused organizations perform so much better than unfocused ones: their processes and values are matched carefully with the set of tasks that need to be done. For these reasons, managers who determine that an organization's capabilities aren't suited for a new task, are faced with three options through which to create new capabilities. They can: · Acquire a different organization whose processes and values are a close match with the new task · Try to change the processes and values of the current organization · Separate out an independent organization and develop within it the new processes and values that are required to solve the new problem Creating Capabilities Through Acquisitions Managers often sense that acquiring rather than developing a set of capabilities makes competitive and financial sense. The RPV model can be a useful way to frame the challenge of integrating acquired organizations. Acquiring managers need to begin by asking, "What is it that really created the value that I just paid so dearly for? Did I justify the price because of its resources—its people, products, technology, market position, and so on? Or, was a substantial portion of its worth created by processes and values—unique ways of working and decision-making that have enabled the company to understand and satisfy customers, and develop, make, and deliver new products and services in a timely way? If the acquired company's processes and values are the real driver of its success, then the last thing the acquiring manager wants to do is to integrate the company into the new parent organization. Integration will vaporize many of the processes and values of the acquired firm as its managers are required to adopt the buyer's way of doing business and have their proposals to innovate evaluated according to the decision criteria of the acquiring company. If the acquiree's processes and values were the reason 137 for its historical success, a better strategy is to let the business stand alone, and for the parent to infuse its resources into the acquired firm's processes and values. This strategy, in essence, truly constitutes the acquisition of new capabilities. If, on the other hand, the company's resources were the primary rationale for the acquisition, then integrating the firm into the parent can make a lot of sense—essentially plugging the acquired people, products, technology, and customers into the parent's processes, as a way of leveraging the parent's existing capabilities. The perils of the DaimlerChrysler merger that began in the late 1990s, for example, can be better understood through the RPV model. Chrysler had few resources that could be considered unique in comparison to its competitors. Its success in the market of the 1990s was rooted in its processes— particularly in its rapid, creative product design processes, and in its processes of integrating the efforts of its subsystem suppliers. What would be the best way for Daimler to leverage the capabilities that Chrysler brought to the table? Wall Street exerted nearly inexorable pressure on management to consolidate the two organizations in order to cut costs. However, integrating the two companies would likely vaporize the key processes that made Chrysler such an attractive acquisition in the first place. This situation is reminiscent of IBM's 1984 acquisition of Rolm. There wasn't anything in Rolm's pool of resources that IBM didn't already have. It was Rolm's processes for developing PBX products and for finding new markets for them that was really responsible for its success. In 1987 IBM decided to fully integrate the company into its corporate structure. Trying to push Rolm's resources—its products and its customers—through the same processes that were honed in its large computer business, caused the Rolm business to stumble badly. And inviting executives of a computer company whose values had been whetted on operating profit margins of 18 percent to get excited about prioritizing products with operating margins below 10 percent was impossible. IBM's decision to integrate Rolm actually destroyed the very source of the original worth of the deal. As this chapter is being written in February 2000, DaimlerChrysler, bowing to the investment community's drumbeat for efficiency savings, now stands on the edge of the same precipice. Often, it seems, financial analysts have a better intuition for the value of resources than for processes. In contrast, Cisco Systems' acquisitions process has worked well—because its managers seem to have kept resources, processes, and values in the right perspective. Between 1993 and 1997 it acquired primarily small companies that were less than two years old: early-stage organizations whose market value was built primarily upon their resources—particularly engineers and products. Cisco has a welldefined, deliberate process by which it essentially plugs these resources into the parent's processes and systems, and it has a carefully cultivated method of keeping the engineers of the acquired company happily on the Cisco payroll. In the process of integration, Cisco throws away whatever nascent processes and values came with the acquisition—because those weren't what Cisco paid for. On a couple of occasions when the company acquired a larger, more mature organization—notably its 1996 acquisition of StrataCom—Cisco did not integrate. Rather, it let StrataCom stand alone, and infused its substantial resources into the organization to help it grow at a more rapid rate.8 On at least three occasions, Johnson & Johnson has used acquisitions to establish a position in an important wave of disruptive technology. Its businesses in disposable contact lenses, endoscopic surgery, and diabetes blood glucose meters were all acquired when they were small, were allowed to stand alone, and were infused with resources. Each has become a billion-dollar business. Lucent Technologies and Nortel followed a similar strategy for catching the wave of routers, based upon packet-switching technology, that were disrupting their traditional circuit-switching equipment. But 138 they made these acquisitions late and the firms they acquired, Ascend Communications and Bay Networks, respectively, were extraordinarily expensive because they had already created the new market application, data networks, along with the much larger Cisco Systems—and they were right on the verge of attacking the voice network. Creating New Capabilities Internally Companies that have tried to develop new capabilities within established organizational units also have a spotty track record, unfortunately. Assembling a beefed-up set of resources as a means of changing what an existing organization can do is relatively straightforward. People with new skills can be hired, technology can be licensed, capital can be raised, and product lines, brands, and information can be acquired. Too often, however, resources such as these are then plugged into fundamentally unchanged processes—and little change results. For example, through the 1970s and 1980s Toyota upended the world automobile industry through its innovation in development, manufacturing, and supply-chain processes—without investing aggressively in resources such as advanced manufacturing or information-processing technology. General Motors responded by investing nearly $60 billion in manufacturing resources—computer-automated equipment that was designed to reduce cost and improve quality. Using state-of-the-art resources in antiquated processes, however, made little difference in General Motors' performance, because it is in its processes and values that the organization's most fundamental capabilities lie. Processes and values define how resources—many of which can be bought and sold, hired and fired—are combined to create value. Unfortunately, processes are very hard to change—for two reasons. The first is that organizational boundaries are often drawn to facilitate the operation of present processes. Those boundaries can impede the creation of new processes that cut across those boundaries. When new challenges require different people or groups to interact differently than they habitually have done—addressing different challenges with different timing than historically had been required—managers need to pull the relevant people out of the existing organization and draw a new boundary around a new group. New team boundaries enable or facilitate new patterns of working together that ultimately can coalesce as new processes—new capabilities for transforming inputs into outputs. Professors Steven C. Wheelwright and Kim B. Clark have called these structures heavyweight teams.9 The second reason new process capabilities are hard to develop is that, in some cases, managers don't want to throw the existing processes out—the methods work perfectly well in doing what they were designed to do. As noted above, while resources tend to be flexible and can be used in a variety of situations, processes and values are by their very nature inflexible. Their very raison d'être is to cause the same thing to be done consistently, over and over again. Processes are meant not to change. When disruptive change appears on the horizon, managers need to assemble the capabilities to confront the change before it has affected the mainstream business. In other words, they need an organization that is geared toward the new challenge before the old one, whose processes are tuned to the existing business model, has reached a crisis that demands fundamental change. Because of its task-specific nature, it is impossible to ask one process to do two fundamentally different things. Consider the examples presented in chapter 7, for instance. The market research and planning processes that are appropriate for the launch of new products into existing markets simply aren't capable of guiding a company into emerging, poorly defined markets. And the processes by which a 139 company would experimentally and intuitively feel its way into emerging markets would constitute suicide if employed in a well-defined existing business. If a company needs to do both types of tasks simultaneously, then it needs two very different processes. And it is very difficult for a single organizational unit to employ fundamentally different, opposing processes. As shown below, this is why managers need to create different teams, within which different processes to address new problems can be defined and refined. Creating Capabilities Through a Spin-out Organization The third mechanism for new capability creation—spawning them within spin-out ventures—is currently en vogue among many managers as they wrestle with how to address the Internet. When are spin-outs a crucial step in building new capabilities to exploit change, and what are the guidelines by which they should be managed? A separate organization is required when the mainstream organization's values would render it incapable of focusing resources on the innovation project. Large organizations cannot be expected to allocate freely the critical financial and human resources needed to build a strong position in small, emerging markets. And it is very difficult for a company whose cost structure is tailored to compete in high-end markets to be profitable in low-end markets as well. When a threatening disruptive technology requires a different cost structure in order to be profitable and competitive, or when the current size of the opportunity is insignificant relative to the growth needs of the mainstream organization, then—and only then—is a spin-out organization a required part of the solution. How separate does the effort need to be? The primary requirement is that the project cannot be forced to compete with projects in the mainstream organization for resources. Because values are the criteria by which prioritization decisions are made, projects that are inconsistent with a company's mainstream values will naturally be accorded lowest priority. Whether the independent organization is physically separate is less important than is its independence from the normal resource allocation process. In our studies of this challenge, we have never seen a company succeed in addressing a change that disrupts its mainstream values absent the personal, attentive oversight of the CEO—precisely because of the power of processes and values and particularly the logic of the normal resource allocation process. Only the CEO can ensure that the new organization gets the required resources and is free to create processes and values that are appropriate to the new challenge. CEOs who view spin-outs as a tool to get disruptive threats off of their personal agendas are almost certain to meet with failure. We have seen no exceptions to this rule. The framework summarized in Figure 8.1 can help managers exploit the capabilities that reside in their current processes and values when that is possible, and to create new ones, when the present organization is incapable. The left axis in measures the extent to which the existing processes—the patterns of interaction, communication, coordination, and decision-making currently used in the organization—are the ones that will get the new job done effectively. If the answer is yes (toward the lower end of the scale), the project manager can exploit the organization's existing processes and organizational structure to succeed. As depicted in the corresponding position on the right axis, functional or lightweight teams, as described by Clark and Wheelwright,10 are useful structures for exploiting existing capabilities. In such teams, the role of the project manager is to facilitate and coordinate work that is largely done within functional organizations. Fitting an Innovation's Requirements with the Organization's Capabilities Note: The left and bottom axes reflect the questions the manager needs to ask about the existing situations. The notes at the right side represents the appropriate response to the situation on the left axis. The notes at the top represent the appropriate response to the manager's answer to the bottom axis.

On the other hand, if the ways of getting work done and of decision-making in the mainstream business would impede rather than facilitate the work of the new team—because different people need to interact with different people about different subjects and with different timing than has habitually been necessary—then a heavyweight team structure is necessary. Heavyweight teams are tools to create new processes—new ways of working together that constitute new capabilities. In these teams, members do not simply represent the interests and skills of their function. They are charged to act like general managers, and reach decisions and make trade-offs for the good of the project. They typically are dedicated and colocated.

managers to assess whether the organization's values will allocate to the new initiative the resources it will need in order to become successful. If there is a poor, disruptive fit, then the mainstream organization's values will accord low priority to the project. Therefore, setting up an autonomous organization within which development and commercialization can occur will be absolutely essential to success. At the other extreme, however, if there is a strong, sustaining fit, then the manager can expect that the energy and resources of the mainstream organization will coalesce behind it. There is no reason for a skunk works or a spin-out in such cases. Region A in Figure 8.1 depicts a situation in which a manager is faced with a breakthrough but sustaining technological change—it fits the organization's values. But it presents the organization with different types of problems to solve and therefore requires new types of interaction and coordination among groups and individuals. The manager needs a heavyweight development team to tackle the new task, but the project can be executed within the mainstream company. This is how Chrysler, Eli Lilly, and Medtronic accelerated their product development cycles so dramatically.11 Heavyweight teams are the organizational mechanism that the managers of IBM's disk drive division used to learn how to 141 integrate components more effectively in their product designs, in order to wring 50 percent higher performance out of the components they used. Microsoft's project to develop and launch its Internet browser was located in the Region A corner of this framework. It represented an extraordinary, difficult managerial achievement that required different people to work together in patterns different than any ever used before within Microsoft. But it was a sustaining technology to the company. Its customers wanted the product, and it strengthened the company's integral business model. There was, therefore, no need to spin the project out into a completely different organization. When in Region B, where the project fits the company's processes and values, a lightweight development team can be successful. In such teams coordination across functional boundaries occurs within the mainstream organization. Region C denotes an area in which a manager is faced with a disruptive technological change that doesn't fit the organization's existing processes and values. To ensure success in such instances, managers should create an autonomous organization and commission a heavyweight development team to tackle the challenge. In addition to the examples cited in chapters 5, 6, and 7, many companies' efforts to address the distribution channel conflicts created by the Internet should be managed in this manner. In 1999 Compaq Computer, for example, launched a business to market its computers direct to customers over the Internet, so that it could compete more effectively with Dell Computer. Within a few weeks its retailers had protested so loudly that Compaq had to back away from the strategy. This was very disruptive to the values, or profit model, of the company and its retailers. The only way it could manage this conflict would be to launch the direct business through an independent company. It might even need a different brand in order to manage the tension. Some have suggested that Wal-Mart's strategy of managing its on-line retailing operation through an independent organization in Silicon Valley is foolhardy, because the spin-out organization can't leverage Wal-Mart's extraordinary logistics management processes and infrastructure. I believe the spin-out was wise, however, based upon Figure 8.1. The on-line venture actually needs very different logistics processes than those of its bricks-and-mortar operations. Those operations transport goods by the truckload. On-line retailers need to pick individual items from inventory and ship small packages to diverse locations. The venture is not only disruptive to Wal-Mart's values, but it needs to create its own logistics processes as well. It needed to be spun out separately. Region D typifies projects in which products or services similar to those in the mainstream need to be sold within a fundamentally lower overhead cost business model. Wal-Mart's Sam's Clubs would fit in this region. These, in fact, can leverage similar logistics management processes as the main company; but budgeting, management, and P&L responsibility needs to be different. Functional and lightweight teams are appropriate vehicles for exploiting established capabilities, whereas heavyweight teams are tools for creating new ones. Spin-out organizations, similarly, are tools for forging new values. Unfortunately, most companies employ a one-size-fits-all organizing strategy, using lightweight teams for programs of every size and character. Among those few firms that have accepted the "heavyweight gospel," many have attempted to organize all of their development teams in a heavyweight fashion. Ideally, each company should tailor the team structure and organizational location to the process and values required by each project. In many ways, the disruptive technologies model is a theory of relativity, because what is disruptive to one company might have a sustaining impact on another. For example, Dell Computer began by selling computers over the telephone. For Dell, the initiative to begin selling and accepting orders over the Internet was a sustaining innovation. It helped it make more money in the way it was already 142 structured. For Compaq, Hewlett-Packard, and IBM, however, marketing direct to customers over the Internet would have a powerfully disruptive impact. The same is true in stock brokerage. For discount brokers such as Ameritrade and Charles Schwab, which accepted most of their orders by telephone, trading securities on-line simply helped them discount more cost-effectively—and even offer enhanced service relative to their former capabilities. For full-service firms with commissioned brokers such as Merrill Lynch, however, on-line trading represents a powerful disruptive threat.

Managers whose organizations are confronting change must first determine that they have the resources required to succeed. They then need to ask a separate question: does the organization have the processes and values to succeed? Asking this second question is not as instinctive for most managers because the processes by which work is done and the values by which employees make their decisions have served them well. What I hope this framework adds to managers' thinking, however, is that the very capabilities of their organizations also define their disabilities. A little time spent soul-searching for honest answers to this issue will pay off handsomely. Are the processes by which work habitually gets done in the organization appropriate for this new problem? And will the values of the organization cause this initiative to get high priority, or to languish? If the answer to these questions is no, it's okay. Understanding problems is the most crucial step in solving them. Wishful thinking about this issue can set teams charged with developing and implementing an innovation on a course fraught with roadblocks, second-guessing, and frustration. The reasons why innovation often seems to be so difficult for established firms is that they employ highly capable people, and then set them to work within processes and values that weren't designed to facilitate success with the task at hand. Ensuring that capable people are ensconced in capable organizations is a major management responsibility in an age such as ours, when the ability to cope with accelerating change has become so critical.

8

Performance Provided, Market Demand, and the Product Life Cycle

The graphs in this book showing the intersecting technology and market trajectories have proven useful in explaining how leading firms can stumble from positions of industry leadership. In each of the several industries explored, technologists were able to provide rates of performance improvement that have exceeded the rates of performance improvement that the market has needed or was able to absorb. Historically, when this performance oversupply occurs, it creates an opportunity for a disruptive technology to emerge and subsequently to invade established markets from below. As it creates this threat or opportunity for a disruptive technology, performance oversupply also triggers a fundamental change in the basis of competition in the product's market: The rank-ordering of the criteria by which customers choose one product or service over another will change, signaling a transition from one phase (variously defined by management theorists) to the next of the product life cycle. In other words, the intersecting trajectories of performance supplied and performance demanded are fundamental triggers behind the phases in the product life cycle. Because of this, trajectory maps such as those used in this book usefully characterize how an industry's competitive dynamics and its basis of competition are likely to change over time. As with past chapters, this discussion begins with an analysis from the disk drive industry of what can happen when the performance supplied exceeds the market's demands.

After seeing the same phenomenon played out in the markets for accounting software and for diabetes care products, the link between this pattern and the phases of the product life cycle will be clear. PERFORMANCE OVERSUPPLY AND CHANGING BASES OF COMPETITION The phenomenon of performance oversupply is charted in Figure 9.1, an extract from Figure 1.7. It shows that by 1988, the capacity of the average 3.5-inch drive had finally increased to equal the capacity demanded in the mainstream desktop personal computer market, and that the capacity of the average 5.25-inch drive had by that time surpassed what the mainstream desktop market demanded by nearly 300 percent. At this point, for the first time since the desktop market emerged, computer makers had a choice of drives to buy: The 5.25- and 3.5-inch drives both provided perfectly adequate capacity. What was the result? The desktop personal computer makers began switching to 3.5-inch drives in droves. Figure 9.2 illustrates this, using a substitution curve format in which the vertical axis measures the ratio of new- to old-technology units sold. In 1985 this measure was .007, meaning that less than 1 percent (.0069) of the desktop market had switched to the 3.5-inch format. By 1987, the ratio had advanced 0.20, meaning that 16.7 percent of the units sold into this market that year were 3.5-inch 145 drives. By 1989, the measure was 1.5, that is, only four years after the 3.5-inch product had appeared as a faint blip on the radar screen of the market, it accounted for 60 percent of drive sales. Why did the 3.5-inch drive so decisively conquer the desktop PC market? A standard economic guess might be that the 3.5-inch format represented a more cost-effective architecture: If there were no longer any meaningful differentiation between two types of products (both had adequate capacity), price competition would intensify. This was not the case here, however. Indeed, computer makers had to pay, on average, 20 percent more per megabyte to use 3.5-inch drives, and yet they still flocked to the product. Moreover, computer manufacturers opted for the costlier drive while facing fierce price competition in their own product markets. Why?

Performance oversupply triggered a change in the basis of competition. Once the demand for capacity was satiated, other attributes, whose performance had not yet satisfied market demands, came to be more highly valued and to constitute the dimensions along which drive makers sought to differentiate their products. In concept, this meant that the most important attribute measured on the vertical axis of figures such as 8.1 changed, and that new trajectories of product performance, compared to market demands, took shape. 146 Specifically, in the desktop personal computer marketplace between 1986 and 1988, the smallness of the drive began to matter more than other features. The smaller 3.5-inch drive allowed computer manufacturers to reduce the size, or desktop footprint, of their machines. At IBM, for example, the large XT/AT box gave way to the much smaller PS1/PS2 generation machines.

For a time, when the availability of small drives did not satisfy market demands, desktop computer makers continued to pay a hefty premium for 3.5-inch drives. In fact, using the hedonic regression analysis described in chapter 4, the 1986 shadow price for a one-cubic-inch reduction in the volume of a disk drive was $4.72. But once the computer makers had configured their new generations of desktop machines to use the smaller drive, their demand for even more smallness was satiated. As a result, the 1989 shadow price, or the price premium accorded to smaller drives, diminished to $0.06 for a onecubic-inch reduction. Generally, once the performance level demanded of a particular attribute has been achieved, customers indicate their satiation by being less willing to pay a premium price for continued improvement in that attribute. Hence, performance oversupply triggers a shift in the basis of competition, and the criteria used by customers to choose one product over another changes to attributes for which market demands are not yet satisfied. Figure 9.3 summarizes what seems to have happened in the desktop PC market: The attribute measured on the vertical axis repeatedly changed. Performance oversupply in capacity triggered the first redefinition of the vertical axis, from capacity to physical size. When performance on this new 147 dimension satisfied market needs, the definition of performance on the vertical axis changed once more, to reflect demand for reliability. For a time, products offering competitively superior shock resistance and mean time between failure (MTBF) were accorded a significant price premium, compared to competitive offerings. But as MTBF values approached one million hours,1 the shadow price accorded to an increment of one hundred hours MTBF approached zero, suggesting performance oversupply on that dimension of product performance. The subsequent and current phase is an intense price-based competition, with gross margins tumbling below 12 percent in some instances. WHEN DOES A PRODUCT BECOME A COMMODITY? The process of commoditization of disk drives was defined by the interplay between the trajectories of what the market demanded and what the technology supplied. The 5.25-inch drive had become a pricedriven commodity in the desktop market by about 1988, when the 3.5-inch drive was still at a premium price. The 5.25-inch drive, in addition, even though priced as a commodity in desktop applications, was at the same time, relative to 8-inch drives, achieving substantial price premiums in higher-tier markets. As described in chapter 4, this explains the aggressive moves upmarket made by established companies.

A product becomes a commodity within a specific market segment when the repeated changes in the basis of competition, as described above, completely play themselves out, that is, when market needs on each attribute or dimension of performance have been fully satisfied by more than one available product. The performance oversupply framework may help consultants, managers, and researchers to understand the frustrated comments they regularly hear from salespeople beaten down in price negotiations with customers: "Those stupid guys are just treating our product like it was a commodity. Can't they see how much better our product is than the competition's?" It may, in fact, be the case that the product offerings of competitors in a market continue to be differentiated from each other. But differentiation loses its meaning when the features and functionality have exceeded what the market demands. PERFORMANCE OVERSUPPLY AND THE EVOLUTION OF PRODUCT COMPETITION The marketing literature provides numerous descriptions of the product life cycle and of the ways in which the characteristics of products within given categories evolve over time.2 The findings in this book suggest that, for many of these models, performance oversupply is an important factor driving the transition from one phase of the cycle to the next.

Consider, for example, the product evolution model, called the buying hierarchy by its creators, Windermere Associates of San Francisco, California, which describes as typical the following four phases: functionality, reliability, convenience, and price. Initially, when no available product satisfies the functionality requirements the market, the basis of competition, or the criteria by which product choice is made, tends to be product functionality. (Sometimes, as in disk drives, a market may cycle through several different functionality dimensions.) Once two or more products credibly satisfy the market's demand for functionality, however, customers can no longer base their choice of products on functionality, but tend to choose a product and vendor based on reliability. As long as market demand for reliability exceeds what vendors are able to provide, customers choose products on this basis—and the most reliable vendors of the most reliable products earn a premium for it. But when two or more vendors improve to the point that they more than satisfy the reliability demanded by the market, the basis of competition shifts to convenience. Customers will prefer those products that are the most convenient to use and those vendors that are most convenient to deal with. Again, as long as the market demand for convenience exceeds what vendors are able to provide, customers choose products on this basis and reward vendors with premium prices for the convenience they offer. Finally, when multiple vendors offer a package of convenient products and services that fully satisfies market demand, the basis of competition shifts to price. The factor driving the transition from one phase of the buying hierarchy to the next is performance oversupply. Another useful conception of industry evolution, formulated by Geoffrey Moore in his book Crossing the Chasm, 3 has a similar underlying logic, but articulates the stages in terms of the user rather than the product. Moore suggests that products are initially used by innovators and early adopters in an industry—customers who base their choice solely on the product's functionality. During this phase the top-performing products command significant price premiums. Moore observes that markets then expand dramatically after the demand for functionality in the mainstream market has been met, and vendors begin to address the need for reliability among what he terms early majority customers. A third wave of growth occurs when product and vendor reliability issues have been resolved, and the basis of innovation and competition shifts to convenience, thus pulling in the late majority customers. Underlying Moore's model is the notion that technology can improve to the point that market demand for a given dimension of performance can be satiated. This evolving pattern in the basis of competition—from functionality, to reliability and convenience, and finally to price—has been seen in many of the markets so far discussed. In fact, a key characteristic of a disruptive technology is that it heralds a change in the basis of competition. OTHER CONSISTENT CHARACTERISTICS OF DISRUPTIVE TECHNOLOGIES Two additional important characteristics of disruptive technologies consistently affect product life cycles and competitive dynamics: First, the attributes that make disruptive products worthless in mainstream markets typically become their strongest selling points in emerging markets; and second, disruptive products tend to be simpler, cheaper, and more reliable and convenient than established products. Managers must understand these characteristics to effectively chart their own strategies for designing, building, and selling disruptive products. Even though the specific market applications for disruptive technologies cannot be known in advance, managers can bet on these two regularities.

The relation between disruptive technologies and the basis of competition in an industry is complex. In the interplay among performance oversupply, the product life cycle, and the emergence of disruptive technologies, it is often the very attributes that render disruptive technologies useless in mainstream markets that constitute their value in new markets. In general, companies that have succeeded in disruptive innovation initially took the characteristics and capabilities of the technology for granted and sought to find or create a new market that would value or accept those attributes. Thus, Conner Peripherals created a market for small drives in portable computers, where smallness was valued; J. C. Bamford and J. I. Case built a market for excavators among residential contractors, where small buckets and tractor mobility actually created value; and Nucor found a market that didn't mind the surface blemishes on its thin-slab-cast sheet steel. The companies toppled by these disruptive technologies, in contrast, each took the established market's needs as given, and did not attempt to market the technology until they felt it was good enough to be valued in the mainstream market. Thus, Seagate's marketers took the firm's early 3.5-inch drives to IBM for evaluation, rather than asking, "Where is the market that would actually value a smaller, lower-capacity drive?" When Bucyrus Erie acquired its Hydrohoe hydraulic excavator line in 1951, its managers apparently did not ask, "Where is the market that actually wants a mobile excavator that can only dig narrow trenches?" They assumed instead that the market needed the largest possible bucket size and the longest possible reach; they jury-rigged the Hydrohoe with cables, pulleys, clutches, and winches and attempted to sell it to general excavation contractors. When U.S. Steel was evaluating continuous thin-slab casting, they did not ask, "Where is the market for low-priced sheet steel with poor surface appearance?" Rather, they took it for granted that the market needed the highest-possible quality of surface finish and invested more capital in a conventional caster. They applied to a disruptive innovation a way of thinking appropriate to a sustaining technology. In the instances studied in this book, established firms confronted with disruptive technology typically viewed their primary development challenge as a technological one: to improve the disruptive technology enough that it suits known markets. In contrast, the firms that were most successful in commercializing a disruptive technology were those framing their primary development challenge as a marketing one: to build or find a market where product competition occurred along dimensions that favored the disruptive attributes of the product.4 It is critical that managers confronting disruptive technology observe this principle. If history is any guide, companies that keep disruptive technologies bottled up in their labs, working to improve them until they suit mainstream markets, will not be nearly as successful as firms that find markets that embrace the attributes of disruptive technologies as they initially stand. These latter firms, by creating a commercial base and then moving upmarket, will ultimately address the mainstream market much more effectively than will firms that have framed disruptive technology as a laboratory, rather than a marketing, challenge. 2. Disruptive Technologies Are Typically Simpler, Cheaper, and More Reliable and Convenient than Established Technologies 151 When performance oversupply has occurred and a disruptive technology attacks the underbelly of a mainstream market, the disruptive technology often succeeds both because it satisfies the market's need for functionality, in terms of the buying hierarchy, and because it is simpler, cheaper, and more reliable and convenient than mainstream products. Recall, for example, the attack of hydraulic excavation technology into the mainstream sewer and general excavation markets recounted in chapter 3. Once hydraulically powered excavators had the strength to handle buckets of 2 to 4 cubic yards of earth (surpassing the performance demanded in mainstream markets), contractors rapidly switched to these products even though the cable-actuated machines were capable of moving even more earth per scoop. Because both technologies provided adequate bucket capacity for their needs, contractors opted for the technology that was most reliable: hydraulics. Because established companies are so prone to push for high-performance, high-profit products and markets, they find it very difficult not to overload their first disruptive products with features and functionality. Hewlett-Packard's experience in designing its 1.3-inch Kittyhawk disk drive teaches just this lesson. Unable to design a product that was truly simple and cheap, Kittyhawk's champions pushed its capacity to the limits of technology and gave it levels of shock resistance and power consumption that would make it competitive as a sustaining product. When very high volume applications for a cheap, simple, single-function, 10 MB drive began to emerge, HP's product was not disruptive enough to catch that wave. Apple committed a similar error in stretching the functionality of its Newton, instead of initially targeting simplicity and reliability. PERFORMANCE OVERSUPPLY IN THE ACCOUNTING SOFTWARE MARKET Intuit, the maker of financial management software, is known primarily for its extraordinarily successful personal financial software package, Quicken. Quicken dominates its market because it is easy and convenient. Its makers pride themselves on the fact that the vast majority of Quicken customers simply buy the program, boot it up on their computers, and begin using it without having to read the instruction manual. Its developers made it so convenient to use, and continue to make it simpler and more convenient, by watching how customers use the product, not by listening to what they or the "experts" say they need. By watching for small hints of where the product might be difficult or confusing to use, the developers direct their energies toward a progressively simpler, more convenient product that provides adequate, rather than superior, functionality.5 Less well known is Intuit's commanding 70 percent share of the North American small business accounting software market.6 Intuit captured that share as a late entrant when it launched Quickbooks, a product based on three simple insights. First, previously available small business accounting packages had been created under the close guidance of certified public accountants and required users to have a basic knowledge of accounting (debits and credits, assets and liabilities, and so on) and to make every journal entry twice (thus providing an audit trail for each transaction). Second, most existing packages offered a comprehensive and sophisticated array of reports and analyses, an array that grew ever more complicated and specialized with each new release as developers sought to differentiate their products by offering greater functionality. And third, 85 percent of all companies in the United States were too small to employ an accountant: The books were kept by the proprietors or by family members, who had no need for or understanding of most of the entries and reports available from mainstream accounting software. They did not know what an audit trail was, let alone sense a need to use one. 152 Scott Cook, Intuit's founder, surmised that most of these small companies were run by proprietors who relied more on their intuition and direct knowledge of the business than on the information contained in accounting reports. In other words, Cook decided that the makers of accounting software for small businesses had overshot the functionality required by that market, thus creating an opportunity for a disruptive software technology that provided adequate, not superior functionality and was simple and more convenient to use. Intuit's disruptive Quickbooks changed the basis of product competition from functionality to convenience and captured 70 percent of its market within two years of its introduction.7 In fact, by 1995 Quickbooks accounted for a larger share of Intuit's revenues than did Quicken. The response of established makers of small business accounting software to Intuit's invasion, quite predictably, has been to move upmarket, continuing to release packages loaded with greater functionality; these focus on specific market subsegments, targeted at sophisticated users of information systems at loftier tiers of the market. Of the three leading suppliers of small business accounting software (each of which claimed about 30 percent of the market in 1992), one has disappeared and one is languishing. The third has introduced a simplified product to counter the success of Quickbooks, but it has claimed only a tiny portion of the market. PERFORMANCE OVERSUPPLY IN THE PRODUCT LIFE CYCLE OF INSULIN Another case of performance oversupply and disruptive technology precipitating a change in the basis of competition—and threatening a change in industry leadership—is found in the worldwide insulin business. In 1922, four researchers in Toronto first successfully extracted insulin from the pancreases of animals and injected it, with miraculous results, into humans with diabetes. Because insulin was extracted from the ground-up pancreases of cows and pigs, improving the purity of insulin (measured in impure parts per million, or ppm) constituted a critical trajectory of performance improvement. Impurities dropped from 50,000 ppm in 1925 to 10,000 ppm in 1950 to 10 ppm in 1980, primarily as the result of persistent investment and effort by the world's leading insulin manufacturer, Eli Lilly and Company. Despite this improvement, animal insulins, which are slightly different from human insulin, caused a fraction of a percent of diabetic patients to build up resistance in their immune systems. Thus, in 1978, Eli Lilly contracted with Genentech to create genetically altered bacteria that could produce insulin proteins that were the structural equivalent of human insulin proteins and 100 percent pure. The project was technically successful, and in the early 1980s, after a nearly $1 billion investment, Lilly introduced its Humulin-brand insulin to the market. Priced at a 25 percent premium over insulins of animal extraction, because of its human equivalence and its purity, Humulin was the first commercial-scale product for human consumption to emerge from the biotechnology industry. The market's response to this technological miracle, however, was tepid. Lilly found it very difficult to sustain a premium price over animal insulin, and the growth in the sales volume of Humulin was disappointingly slow. "In retrospect," noted a Lilly researcher, "the market was not terribly dissatisfied with pork insulin. In fact, it was pretty happy with it."8 Lilly had spent enormous capital and organizational energy overshooting the market's demand for product purity. Once again, this was a differentiated product to which the market did not accord a price premium because the performance it provided exceeded what the market demanded. 153 Meanwhile, Novo, a much smaller Danish insulin maker, was busy developing a line of insulin pens, a more convenient way for taking insulin. Conventionally, people with diabetes carried a separate syringe, inserted its needle into one glass insulin vial, pulled its plunger out to draw slightly more than the desired amount of insulin into the syringe, and held up the needle and flicked the syringe several times to dislodge any air bubbles that clung to the cylinder walls. They generally then had to repeat this process with a second, slower acting type of insulin. Only after squeezing the plunger slightly to force any remaining bubbles—and, inevitably, some insulin—out of the syringe could they inject themselves with the insulin. This process typically took one to two minutes. Novo's pen, in contrast, held a cartridge containing a couple of weeks' supply of insulin, usually mixtures of both the fast-acting and the gradually released types. People using the Novo pen simply had to turn a small dial to the amount of insulin they needed to inject, poke the pen's needle under the skin, and press a button. The procedure took less than ten seconds. In contrast to Lilly's struggle to command a premium price for Humulin, Novo's convenient pens easily sustained a 30 percent price premium per unit of insulin. Through the 1980s, propelled largely by the success of its line of pens and pre-mixed cartridges, Novo increased its share of the worldwide insulin market substantially—and profitably. Lilly's and Novo's experiences offer further proof that a product whose performance exceeds market demands suffers commodity-like pricing, while disruptive products that redefine the basis of competition command a premium. Teaching the Harvard Business School case to executives and MBA students about Lilly overshooting the market demand for insulin purity has been one of my most interesting professional experiences. In every class, the majority of students quickly pounce on Lilly for having missed something so obvious—that only a fraction of a percent of people with diabetes develop insulin resistance—and that the differentiation between highly purified pork insulin at 10 ppm and perfectly pure Humulin was not significant. Surely, they assert, a few simple focus groups in which patients and doctors were asked whether they wanted purer insulin would have given Lilly adequate guidance. In every discussion, however, more thoughtful students soon begin to sway class opinion toward the view that (as we have seen over and over) what is obvious in retrospect might not be at all obvious in the thick of battle. Of all the physicians to whom Lilly's marketers listened, for example, which ones tended to carry the most credibility? Endocrinologists whose practices focused on diabetes care, the leading customers in this business. What sorts of patients are most likely to consume the professional interests of these specialists? Those with the most advanced and intractable problems, among which insulin resistance was prominent. What, therefore, were these leading customers likely to tell Lilly's marketers when they asked what should be done to improve the next-generation insulin product? Indeed, the power and influence of leading customers is a major reason why companies' product development trajectories overshoot the demands of mainstream markets. Furthermore, thoughtful students observe that it would not even occur to most marketing managers to ask the question of whether a 100 percent pure human insulin might exceed market needs. For more than fifty years in a very successful company with a very strong culture, greater purity was the very definition of a better product. Coming up with purer insulins had always been the formula for staying ahead of the competition. Greater purity had always been a catching story that the salesforce could use to attract the time and attention of busy physicians. What in the company's history would cause its culture-based assumptions suddenly to change and its executives to begin asking questions that never before had needed to be answered?

A second alternative, labeled strategy 2, is to march in lock-step with the needs of customers in a given tier of the market, catching successive waves of change in the basis of competition. Historically, this appears to have been difficult to do, for all of the reasons described in earlier chapters. In the personal computer industry, for example, as the functionality of desktop machines came to satiate the demands of the lower tiers of the market, new entrants such as Dell and Gateway 2000 entered with value 155 propositions centered on convenience of purchase and use. In the face of this, Compaq responded by actively pursuing this second approach, aggressively fighting any upmarket drift by producing a line of computers with low prices and modest functionality targeted to the needs of the lower tiers of the market. The third strategic option for dealing with these dynamics is to use marketing initiatives to steepen the slopes of the market trajectories so that customers demand the performance improvements that the technologists provide. Since a necessary condition for the playing out of these dynamics is that the slope of the technology trajectory be steeper than the market's trajectory, when the two slopes are parallel, performance oversupply—and the progression from one stage of the product life cycle to the next—does not occur or is at least postponed. Some computer industry observers believe that Microsoft, Intel, and the disk drive companies have pursued this last strategy very effectively. Microsoft has used its industry dominance to create and successfully market software packages that consume massive amounts of disk memory and require ever-faster microprocessors to execute. It has, essentially, increased the slopes of the trajectories of improvement in functionality demanded by their customers to parallel the slope of improvement provided by their technologists. The effect of this strategy is described in Figure 9.5, depicting recent events in the disk drive industry.

Notice how the trajectories of capacity demanded in the mid-range, desktop, and notebook computer segments kinked upward in the 1990s along a path that essentially paralleled the capacity path blazed by the makers of 3.5-inch and 2.5-inch disk drives. Because of this, these markets have not experienced performance oversupply in recent years. The 2.5-inch drive remains locked within the notebook computer market because capacity demanded on the desktop is increasing at too brisk a pace. The 3.5-inch drive remains solidly ensconced in the desktop market, and the 1.8-inch drive has penetrated few notebook computers, for the same reasons. In this situation, the companies whose products are positioned closest to the top of the market, such as Seagate and IBM, have been the most profitable, because in the absence of technology oversupply, a shift in the stages of the product life cycle at the high end of the market has been held at bay.

It is unclear how long the marketers at Microsoft, Intel, and Seagate can succeed in creating demand for whatever functionality their technologists can supply. Microsoft's Excel spreadsheet software, for example, required 1.2 MB of disk storage capacity in its version 1.2, released in 1987. Its version 5.0, released in 1995, required 32 MB of disk storage capacity. Some industry observers believe that if a team of developers were to watch typical users, they would find that functionality has substantially overshot mainstream market demands. If true, this could create an opportunity for a disruptive technology—applets picked off the internet and used in simple internet appliances rather than in fullfunction computers, for example—to invade this market from below. RIGHT AND WRONG STRATEGIES Which of the strategies illustrated in Figure 9.4 is best? This study finds clear evidence that there is no one best strategy. Any of the three, consciously pursued, can be successful. Hewlett-Packard's pursuit of the first strategy in its laser jet printer business has been enormously profitable. In this instance, it has been a safe strategy as well, because HP is attacking its own position with disruptive ink-jet technology. Compaq Computer and the trinity of Intel, Microsoft, and the disk drive makers have successfully—at least to date—implemented the second and third strategies, respectively. These successful practitioners have in common their apparent understanding—whether explicit or intuitive—of both their customers' trajectories of need and their own technologists' trajectories of 157 supply. Understanding these trajectories is the key to their success thus far. But the list of firms that have consistently done this is disturbingly short. Most well-run companies migrate unconsciously to the northeast, setting themselves up to be caught by a change in the basis of competition and an attack from below by disruptive technology.

9

Managing Disruptive Technological Change: A Case Study

As we approach the end of this book, we should better understand why great companies can stumble. Incompetence, bureaucracy, arrogance, tired executive blood, poor planning, and short-term investment horizons obviously have played leading roles in toppling many companies. But we have learned here that even the best managers are subject to certain laws that make disruptive innovation difficult. It is when great managers haven't understood or have attempted to fight these forces that their companies have stumbled. This chapter uses the forces and principles described in earlier chapters to illustrate how managers can succeed when faced with disruptive technology change. To do so, I employ a case study format, using a personal voice, to suggest how I, as a hypothetical employee of a major automaker, might manage a program to develop and commercialize one of the most vexing innovations of our day: the electric vehicle. My purpose here is explicitly not to offer any so-called right answer to this particular challenge, nor to predict whether or how electric vehicles may become commercially successful. Rather, it is to suggest in a familiar but challenging context how managers might structure their thinking about a similar problem by proposing a sequence of questions that, if asked, can lead to a sound and useful answer. HOW CAN WE KNOW IF A TECHNOLOGY IS DISRUPTIVE? Electric-powered vehicles have hovered at the fringe of legitimacy since the early 1900s, when they lost the contest for the dominant vehicle design to gasoline power. Research on these vehicles accelerated during the 1970s, however, as policy makers increasingly looked to them as a way to reduce urban air pollution. The California Air Resources Board (CARB) forced an unprecedented infusion of resources into the effort in the early 1990s when it mandated that, starting in 1998, no automobile manufacturer would be allowed to sell any cars in California if electric vehicles did not constitute at least 2 percent of its unit sales in the state.1 In my hypothetical responsibility for managing an automaker's program, my first step would be to ask a series of questions: How much do we need to worry about electric cars? That is, aside from California's mandate, does the electric car pose a legitimate disruptive threat to companies making gasoline-powered automobiles? Does it constitute an opportunity for profitable growth? To answer these questions, I would graph the trajectories of performance improvement demanded in the market versus the performance improvement supplied by the technology; in other words, I would create for electric vehicles a trajectory map similar to those in Figures 1.7 or 9.5. Such charts are the best method I know for identifying disruptive technologies. 160 The first step in making this chart involves defining current mainstream market needs and comparing them with the current capacity of electric vehicles. To measure market needs, I would watch carefully what customers do, not simply listen to what they say. Watching how customers actually use a product provides much more reliable information than can be gleaned from a verbal interview or a focus group.2 Thus, observations indicate that auto users today require a minimum cruising range (that is, the distance that can be driven without refueling) of about 125 to 150 miles; most electric vehicles only offer a minimum cruising range of 50 to 80 miles. Similarly, drivers seem to require cars that accelerate from 0 to 60 miles per hour in less than 10 seconds (necessary primarily to merge safely into highspeed traffic from freeway entrance ramps); most electric vehicles take nearly 20 seconds to get there. And, finally, buyers in the mainstream market demand a wide array of options, but it would be impossible for electric vehicle manufacturers to offer a similar variety within the small initial unit volumes that will characterize that business.3 According to almost any definition of functionality used for the vertical axis of our proposed chart, the electric vehicle will be deficient compared to a gasolinepowered car. This information is not sufficient to characterize electric vehicles as disruptive, however. They will only be disruptive if we find that they are also on a trajectory of improvement that might someday make them competitive in parts of the mainstream market. To assess this possibility, we need to project trajectories measuring the performance improvement demanded in the market versus the performance improvement that electric vehicle technology may provide. If these trajectories are parallel, then electric vehicles are unlikely to become factors in the mainstream market; but if the technology will progress faster than the pace of improvement demanded in the market, then the threat of disruption is real. Figure 10.1 shows that the trajectories of performance improvement demanded in the market—whether measured in terms of required acceleration, cruising range, or top cruising speed—are relatively flat. This is because traffic laws impose a limit on the usefulness of ever-more-powerful cars, and demographic, economic, and geographic considerations limit the increase in commuting miles for the average driver to less than 1 percent per year.4 At the same time, the performance of electric vehicles is improving at a faster rate—between 2 and 4 percent per year—suggesting that sustaining technological advances might indeed carry electric vehicles from their position today, where they cannot compete in mainstream markets, to a position in the future where they might.5 In other words, as an automotive company executive, I would worry about the electric vehicle, not just because it is politically correct to be investing in environmentally friendly technologies, but because electric vehicles have the smell of a disruptive technology. They can't be used in mainstream markets; they offer a set of attributes that is orthogonal to those that command attention in the gasoline-powered value network; and the technology is moving ahead at a faster rate than the market's trajectory of need. Because electric vehicles are not sustaining innovations, however, mainstream automakers naturally doubt that there is a market for them—another symptom of a disruptive innovation. Consider this statement by the director of Ford's electric vehicle program: "The electric Ranger will sell at approximately $30,000 and have a lead-acid battery that will give it a range of 50 miles . . . . The 1998 electric vehicle will be a difficult sell. The products that will be available will not meet customer expectations in terms of range, cost or utility."6 Indeed, given their present performance along these parameters, it will be about as easy to sell electric vehicles into the mainstream car market as it was to sell 5.25-inch disk drives to mainframe computer makers in 1980.

In evaluating these trajectories, I would be careful to keep asking the right question: Will the trajectory of electric vehicle performance ever intersect the trajectory of market demands (as revealed in the way customers use cars)? Industry experts may contend that electric vehicles will never perform as well as gasoline-powered cars, in effect comparing the trajectories of the two technologies. They are probably correct. But, recalling the experience of their counterparts in the disk drive industry, they will have the right answer to the wrong question. I also would note, but not be deterred by, the mountain of expert opinion averring that without a major technological breakthrough in battery technology, there will never be a substantial market for electric vehicles. The reason? If electric vehicles are viewed as a sustaining technology for established market value networks, they are clearly right. But because the track records of experts predicting the nature and size of markets for disruptive technologies is very poor, I would be particularly skeptical of the experts' skepticism, even as I remain uncertain about my own conclusions.

WHERE IS THE MARKET FOR ELECTRIC VEHICLES? 162 Having decided that electric vehicles are a potentially disruptive technology, my next challenge would be to define a marketing strategy that could lead my company to a legitimate, unsubsidized market in which electric cars might first be used. In formulating this marketing strategy, I would apply three findings from earlier chapters in this book. First, I would acknowledge that, by definition, electric vehicles cannot initially be used in mainstream applications because they do not satisfy the basic performance requirements of that market. I would therefore be sure that everybody having anything to do with my program understands this point: Although we don't have a clue about where the market is, the one thing we know for certain is that it isn't in an established automobile market segment. Ironically, I would expect most automakers to focus precisely and myopically on the mainstream market because of the principle of resource dependence and the principle that small markets don't solve the growth and profit needs of big companies. I would not, therefore, follow the lead of other automakers in my search for customers, because I would recognize that their instincts and capabilities are likely to be trained on the wrong target.7 Nonetheless, my task is to find a market in which the vehicles can be used, because the early entrants into disruptive technology markets develop capabilities that constitute strong advantages over later entrants. They're the ones that, from a profitable business base in this beachhead market, will most successfully throw impetus behind the sustaining innovations required to move the disruptive technology upmarket, toward the mainstream. Holding back from the market, waiting for laboratory researchers to develop a breakthrough battery technology, for example, is the path of least resistance for managers. But this strategy has rarely proven to be a viable route to success with a disruptive innovation. Historically, as we have seen, the very attributes that make disruptive technologies uncompetitive in mainstream markets actually count as positive attributes in their emerging value network. In disk drives, the smallness of 5.25-inch models made them unusable in large computers but very useful on the desktop. While the small bucket capacity and short reach of early hydraulic excavators made them useless in general excavation, their ability to dig precise, narrow trenches made them useful in residential construction. Odd as it sounds, therefore, I would direct my marketers to focus on uncovering somewhere a group of buyers who have an undiscovered need for a vehicle that accelerates relatively slowly and can't be driven farther than 100 miles! The second point on which I would base my marketing approach is that no one can learn from market research what the early market(s) for electric vehicles will be. I can hire consultants, but the only thing I can know for sure is that their findings will be wrong. Nor can customers tell me whether or how they might use electric vehicles, because they will discover how they might use the products at the same time as we discover it—just as Honda's Supercub opened an unforeseen new application for motorbiking. The only useful information about the market will be what I create through expeditions into the market, through testing and probing, trial and error, by selling real products to real people who pay real money.8 Government mandates, incidentally, are likely to distort rather than solve the problem of finding a market. I would, therefore, force my organization to live by its wits rather than to rely on capricious subsidies or non-economic–based California regulation to fuel my business. The third point is that my business plan must be a plan for learning, not one for executing a preconceived strategy. Although I will do my best to hit the right market with the right product and the right strategy the first time out, there is a high probability that a better direction will emerge as the business heads toward its initial target. I must therefore plan to be wrong and to learn what is right as fast as possible.9 I cannot spend all of my resources or all of my organizational credibility on an all-or- 163 nothing first-time bet, as Apple did with its Newton or Hewlett-Packard did with its Kittyhawk. I need to conserve resources to get it right on the second or third try. These three concepts would constitute the foundation of my marketing strategy.

Potential Markets: Some Speculation What might emerge as the initial value network for electric vehicles? Again, though it is impossible to predict, it almost surely will be one in which the weaknesses of the electric vehicle will be seen as strengths. One of my students has suggested that the parents of high school students, who buy their children cars for basic transportation to and from school, friends' homes, and school events, might constitute a fertile market for electric vehicles.10 Given the option, these parents might see the product simplicity, slow acceleration, and limited driving range of electric vehicles as very desirable attributes for their teenagers' cars—especially if they were styled with teenagers in mind. Given the right marketing approach, who knows what might happen? An earlier generation met a lot of nice people on their Hondas. Another possible early market might be taxis or small-parcel delivery vehicles destined for the growing, crowded, noisy, polluted cities of Southeast Asia. Vehicles can sit on Bangkok's roads all day, mostly idling in traffic jams and never accelerating above 30 miles per hour. Electric motors would not need to run and hence would not drain the battery while idling. The maneuverability and ease of parking of these small vehicles would be additional attractions. These or similar market ideas, whether or not they ultimately prove viable, are at least consistent with the way disruptive technologies develop and emerge. How Are Today's Automobile Companies Marketing Electric Vehicles? The strategy proposed here for finding and defining the initial market for electric vehicles stands in stark contrast to the marketing approaches being used by today's major automakers, each of which is struggling to sell electric vehicles into its mainstream market in the time-honored tradition of established firms mishandling disruptive technologies. Consider this statement made in 1995 by William Glaub, Chrysler general sales manager, discussing his company's planned offering for 1998.11 Chrysler Corporation is preparing to provide an electric powered version of our slick new minivan in time for the 1998 model year. After an in-depth study of the option between a purpose-built vehicle and modification of an existing platform, the choice of the minivan to use as an electric powered platform, in retrospect, is an obvious best choice for us. Our experience shows that fleets will likely be the best opportunity to move any number of these vehicles . . . . The problem that we face is not in creating an attractive package. The new minivan is an attractive package. The problem is that sufficient energy storage capacity is not available on board the vehicle.12 To position its offering in the mainstream market, Chrysler has had to pack its minivan with 1,600 pounds of batteries. This, of course, makes its acceleration much slower, its driving range shorter, and 164 its braking distance longer than other available gasoline-powered automobiles. Because of the way Chrysler has positioned its electric vehicle, industry analysts naturally compare it to gasoline-powered minivans, using the metrics paramount in the mainstream value network. At an estimated cost of $100,000 (compared with $22,000 for the gasoline-powered model), nobody in their right mind would consider buying Chrysler's product. Chrysler's marketers are, naturally enough, very pessimistic about their ability to sell any electric minivans in California, despite the government's mandate that they do so. William Glaub, for example, continued the remarks cited above with the following observation: Markets are developed with fine products that customers desire to own. No salesman can take marginal product into the marketplace and have any hope of establishing a sustainable consumer base. Consumers will not be forced into a purchase that they do not want. Mandates will not work in a consumer-driven, free market economy. For electric vehicles to find a place in the market, respectable products comparable to today's gasoline-powered cars must be available.13 Chrysler's conclusion is absolutely correct, given the way its marketers have framed their challenge.14 Mainstream customers can never use a disruptive technology at its outset. WHAT SHOULD BE OUR PRODUCT, TECHNOLOGY, AND DISTRIBUTION STRATEGIES? Product Development for Disruptive Innovations Guiding my engineers in designing our initial electric vehicle will be a challenge, because of the classic chicken-and-egg problem: Without a market, there is no obvious or reliable source of customer input; without a product that addresses customers' needs, there can be no market. How can we design a product in such a vacuum? Fortunately, the principles described in this book give us some help. The most valuable guidance comes from chapter 9, which indicated that the basis of competition will change over a product's life cycle and that the cycle of evolution itself is driven by the phenomenon of performance oversupply, that is, the condition in which the performance provided by a technology exceeds the actual needs of the market. Historically, performance oversupply opens the door for simpler, less expensive, and more convenient—and almost always disruptive—technologies to enter. Performance oversupply indeed seems to have occurred in autos. There are practical limits to the size of auto bodies and engines, to the value of going from 0 to 60 in fewer seconds, and to the consumer's ability to cope with overchoice in available options. Thus, we can safely predict that the basis of product competition and customer choice will shift away from these measures of functionality toward other attributes, such as reliability and convenience. This is borne out by the nature of the most successful entrants into the North American market during the past thirty years; they have succeeded not because they introduced products with superior functionality, but because they competed on the basis of reliability and convenience. Toyota, for example, entered the U.S. market with its simple, reliable Corona, establishing a low-end market position. Then, consistent with the inexorable attraction to migrate upmarket, Toyota introduced 165 models, such as Camry, Previa, and Lexus, with added features and functionality, creating a vacuum at the low end of the market into which entrants such as Saturn and Hyundai have entered. Saturn's strategy has been to characterize the customer's entire experience of buying and owning the vehicle as reliable and convenient, but it, too, judging by recent reports,15 will soon take its turn moving upmarket, creating a new vacuum at the low end for even simpler, more convenient transportation. In all likelihood, therefore, the winning design in the first stages of the electric vehicle race will be characterized by simplicity and convenience and will be incubated in an emerging value network in which these attributes are important measures of value. Each of the disruptive technologies studied in this book has been smaller, simpler, and more convenient than preceding products. Each was initially used in a new value network in which simplicity and convenience were valued. This was true for smaller, simpler disk drives; desktop and portable computers; hydraulic backhoes; steel minimills as opposed to integrated mills; insulin-injecting pens as opposed to syringes.16 Using these qualities as my guiding principles, I would instruct my design engineers to proceed according to the following three criteria. First, this vehicle must be simple, reliable, and convenient. That probably means, for example, that figuring out a way to recharge its batteries quickly, using the commonly available electrical service, would be an immutable technological objective. Second, because no one knows the ultimate market for the product or how it will ultimately be used, we must design a product platform in which feature, function, and styling changes can be made quickly and at low cost. Assuming, for example, that the initial customers for electric vehicles will be parents who buy them for their teenaged children to drive to and from school, friends' homes, and activities, the first model would have features and styling appropriate and appealing to teenagers. But, although we may target this market first, there's a high probability that our initial concept will prove wrong. So we've got to get the first models done fast and on a shoestring—leaving ample budget to get it right once feedback from the market starts coming in.17 Third, we must hit a low price point. Disruptive technologies typically have a lower sticker price per unit than products that are used in the mainstream, even though their cost in use is often higher. What enabled the use of disk drives in desktop computers was not just their smaller size; it was their low unit price, which fit within the overall price points that personal computer makers needed to hit. The price per megabyte of the smaller disk drives was always higher than for the larger drives. Similarly, in excavators the price per excavator was lower for the early hydraulic models than for the established cable-actuated ones, but their total cost per cubic yard of earth moved per hour was much higher. Accordingly, our electric vehicle must have a lower sticker price than the prevailing price for gasolinepowered cars, even if the operating cost per mile driven is higher. Customers have a long track record of paying price premiums for convenience. Technology Strategy for Disruptive Innovations Our technology plan cannot call for any technological breakthroughs on the path critical for the project's success. Historically, disruptive technologies involve no new technologies; rather, they consist of components built around proven technologies and put together in a novel product architecture that offers the customer a set of attributes never before available. 166 The major automakers engaged in electric vehicle development today all maintain that a breakthrough in battery technology is absolutely essential before electric vehicles can be commercially viable. John R. Wallace, of Ford, for example, has stated the following: The dilemma is that today's batteries cannot satisfy these consumer needs. As anybody who is familiar with today's battery technology will tell you, electric vehicles are not ready for prime time. All of the batteries expected to be available in 1998 fall short of the 100-mile range [required by consumers]. The only solution for the problems of range and cost is improved battery technology. To ensure a commercially successful electric vehicle market, the focus of our resources should be on the development of battery technology. Industry efforts such as those through the U.S. Advanced Battery consortium, along with cooperative efforts among all electric vehicle stakeholders—such as utilities, battery companies, environmentalists, regulators and converters—are the most effective way to ensure the marketability of electric vehicles.18 William Glaub, of Chrysler, takes a similar position: "The advanced lead-acid batteries that will be used will provide less than the fuel storage equivalent of two gallons of gasoline. This is like leaving home every day with the 'low fuel' light on. In other words, the battery technology is simply not ready."19 The reason these companies view a breakthrough in battery technology as the critical bottleneck to the commercial success of electric vehicles, of course, is that their executives have positioned their minds and their products in the mainstream market. For Chrysler, this means an electric minivan; for Ford, an electric Ranger. Given this position, they must deliver a sustaining technological impact from what is inherently a disruptive technology. They need a breakthrough in battery technology because they made the choice to somehow position electric vehicles as a sustaining technology. A battery breakthrough is not likely to be required of companies whose executives choose to harness or account for the basic laws of disruptive technology by creating a market in which the weaknesses of the electric vehicle become its strengths. Where will advances in battery technology eventually come from? Looking at the historical record, we can assert the following. The companies that ultimately achieve the advances in battery technology required to power cars for 150-mile cruises (if they are ever developed) will be those that pioneer the creation of a new value network using proven technology and then develop the sustaining technologies needed to carry them upward into more attractive markets.20 Our finding that well-managed companies are generally upwardly mobile and downwardly immobile, therefore, suggests that the impetus to find the battery breakthrough will indeed be strongest among the disruptive innovators, which will have built a low-end market for electric vehicles before trying to move upmarket toward the larger, more profitable mainstream. Distribution Strategy for Disruptive Innovations It has almost always been the case that disruptive products redefine the dominant distribution channels, because dealers' economics—their models for how to make money—are powerfully shaped by the mainstream value network, just as the manufacturer's are. Sony's disruptive introduction of convenient and reliable portable transistorized radios and televisions shifted the dominant retail channel from appliance and department stores with expensive sales support and field service networks (required for 167 sets built with vacuum tubes) to volume-oriented, low-overhead discount retailers. Honda's disruptive motorbikes were rejected by mainstream motorcycle dealers, forcing the company to create a new channel among sporting goods retailers. We saw, in fact, that a major reason why Harley-Davidson's small-bike initiative failed is that its dealers rejected it: The image and economics of the small Italian bikes Harley had acquired did not fit its dealer network. The reason disruptive technologies and new distribution channels frequently go hand-in-hand is, in fact, an economic one. Retailers and distributors tend to have very clear formulas for making money, as the histories of Kresge and Woolworth in chapter 4 showed. Some make money by selling low volumes of big-ticket products at high margins; others make money by selling large volumes at razor-thin margins that cover minimal operating overheads; still others make their money servicing products already sold. Just as disruptive technologies don't fit the models of established firms for improving profits, they often don't fit the models of their distributors, either. My electric vehicle program would, therefore, have as a basic strategic premise the need to find or create new distribution channels for electric vehicles. Unless proven otherwise, I'd bet that mainstream dealers of gasoline-powered automobiles would not view the sorts of disruptive electric vehicles we have in mind as critical to their success. WHAT ORGANIZATION BEST SERVES DISRUPTIVE INNOVATIONS? After identifying the electric vehicle as a potentially disruptive technology; setting realistic bearings for finding its potential markets; and establishing strategic parameters for the product's design, technology, and distribution network, as program manager I would next turn to organization. Creating an organizational context in which this effort can prosper will be crucial, because rational resource allocation processes in established companies consistently deny disruptive technologies the resources they need to survive, regardless of the commitment senior management may ostensibly have made to the program. Spinning Off an Independent Organization As we saw in the discussion of resource dependence in chapter 5, established firms that successfully built a strong market position in a disruptive technology were those that spun off from the mainstream company an independent, autonomously operated organization. Quantum, Control Data, IBM's PC Division, Allen Bradley, and Hewlett-Packard's desk-jet initiative all succeeded because they created organizations whose survival was predicated upon successful commercialization of the disruptive technology: These firms embedded a dedicated organization squarely within the emerging value network. As program manager, therefore, I would strongly urge corporate management to create an independent organization to commercialize electric vehicle technology, either an autonomous business unit, such as GM's Saturn

Division or the IBM PC Division, or an independent company whose stock is largely owned by the corporation. In an independent organization, my best employees would be able to focus on electric vehicles without being repeatedly withdrawn from the project to solve pressing problems for 168 customers who pay the present bills. Demands from our own customers, on the other hand, would help us to focus on and lend impetus and excitement to our program. An independent organization would not only make resource dependence work for us rather than against us, but it would also address the principle that small markets cannot solve the growth or profit problems of large companies. For many years into the future, the market for electric vehicles will be so small that this business is unlikely to contribute significantly to the top or bottom lines of a major automaker's income statement. Thus, since senior managers at these companies cannot be expected to focus either their priority attention or their priority resources on electric vehicles, the most talented managers and engineers would be unlikely to want to be associated with our project, which must inevitably be seen as a financially insignificant effort: To secure their own futures within the company, they naturally will want to work on mainstream programs, not peripheral ones. In the early years of this new business, orders are likely to be denominated in hundreds, not tens of thousands. If we are lucky enough to get a few wins, they almost surely will be small ones. In a small, independent organization, these small wins will generate energy and enthusiasm. In the mainstream, they would generate skepticism about whether we should even be in the business. I want my organization's customers to answer the question of whether we should be in the business. I don't want to spend my precious managerial energy constantly defending our existence to efficiency analysts in the mainstream. Innovations are fraught with difficulties and uncertainties. Because of this, I want always to be sure that the projects that I manage are positioned directly on the path everyone believes the organization must take to achieve higher growth and greater profitability. If my program is widely viewed as being on that path, then I have confidence that when the inevitable problems arise, somehow the organization will work with me to muster whatever it takes to solve them and succeed. If, on the other hand, my program is viewed by key people as nonessential to the organization's growth and profitability, or even worse, is viewed as an idea that might erode profits, then even if the technology is simple, the project will fail. I can address this challenge in one of two ways: I could convince everyone in the mainstream (in their heads and their guts) that the disruptive technology is profitable, or I could create an organization that is small enough, with an appropriate cost structure, that my program can be viewed as being on its critical path to success. The latter alternative is a far more tractable management challenge. In a small, independent organization I will more likely be able to create an appropriate attitude toward failure. Our initial stab into the market is not likely to be successful. We will, therefore, need the flexibility to fail, but to fail on a small scale, so that we can try again without having destroyed our credibility. Again, there are two ways to create the proper tolerance toward failure: change the values and culture of the mainstream organization or create a new organization. The problem with asking the mainstream organization to be more tolerant of risk-taking and failure is that, in general, we don't want to tolerate marketing failure when, as is most often the case, we are investing in sustaining technology change. The mainstream organization is involved in taking sustaining technological innovations into existing markets populated by known customers with researchable needs. Getting it wrong the first time is not an intrinsic part of these processes: Such innovations are amenable to careful planning and coordinated execution. Finally, I don't want my organization to have pockets that are too deep. While I don't want my people to feel pressure to generate significant profit for the mainstream company (this would force us into a fruitless search for an instant large market), I want them to feel constant pressure to find some way— some set of customers somewhere—to make our small organization cash-positive as fast as possible.

We need a strong motivation to accelerate through the trials and errors inherent in cultivating a new market. Of course, the danger in making this unequivocal call for spinning out an independent company is that some managers might apply this remedy indiscriminately, viewing skunkworks and spinoffs as a blanket solution—an industrial-strength aspirin that cures all sorts of problems. In reality, spinning out is an appropriate step only when confronting disruptive innovation. The evidence is very strong that large, mainstream organizations can be extremely creative in developing and implementing sustaining innovations.21 In other words, the degree of disruptiveness inherent in an innovation provides a fairly clear indication of when a mainstream organization might be capable of succeeding with it and when it might be expected to fail. In this context, the electric vehicle is not only a disruptive innovation, but it involves massive architectural reconfiguration as well, a reconfiguration that must occur not only within the product itself but across the entire value chain. From procurement through distribution, functional groups will have to interface differently than they have ever before. Hence, my project would need to be managed as a heavyweight team in an organization independent of the mainstream company. This organizational structure cannot guarantee the success of our electric vehicle program, but it would at least allow my team to work in an environment that accounts for, rather than fights, the principles of disruptive innovation.